Easy Walks and Paddles in the Ten Mile River Watershed

Attleboro, North Attleboro, Plainville,
Seekonk, MA,
and
East Providence, Pawtucket, RI

Edited by Marjorie Turner Hollman

Copyright © April 2018 The Ten Mile River Watershed Council

Published by MarjorieTurner.com

ISBN-13:978-1985377011
ISBN-10:1985377012

Please do not copy or distribute this copyrighted book. Copies are available on Amazon.com or from the publisher.

Maps produced using information from the U.S. Geological Survey

Digital icons open sourced from clker.com

Easy Walks and Paddles in the Ten Mile River Watershed: Attleboro, North Attleboro, Plainville, Seekonk, MA and East Providence, Pawtucket, RI

1. Non-fiction 2. Sports and Recreation 3. Hiking 4. Biking 5. Kayaking; 6. Family activities, 7. Southern New England outdoor activities

Disclaimer: The author and contributors to this book make no representation of accuracy of content, nor guarantee rights of access to any places described herein. Users of this book indemnify and hold harmless the author and contributors.

"This publication is supported in part by a grant from the Seekonk, North Attleboro and Plainville, MA Cultural Councils, local agencies which are supported by the Mass Cultural Council, a state agency."

MarjorieTurner.com

Bellingham, MA 02019

Towns of the Watershed

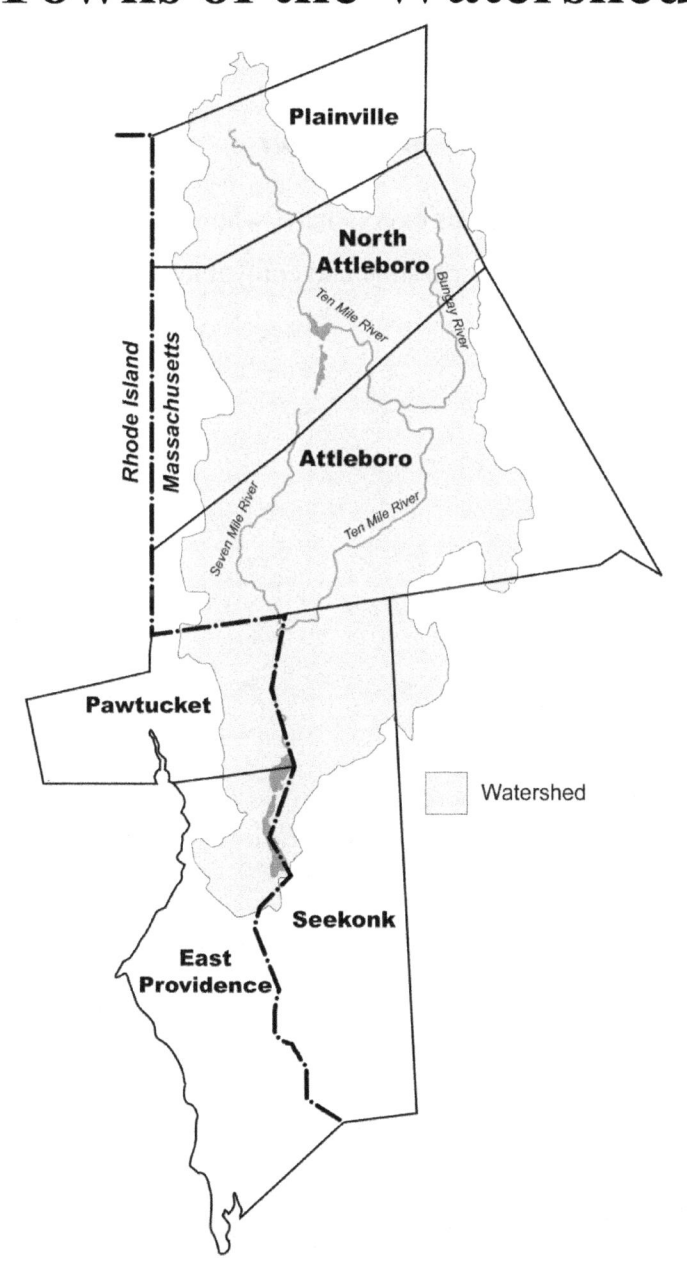

Dedication

For all the water protectors everywhere, who work tirelessly to make our waterways accessible and enjoyable for everyone.

Table of Contents

Easy Walks and Paddles in the Ten Mile River Watershed ...i

    Attleboro, North Attleboro, Plainville, Seekonk, MA, and East Providence, Pawtucket, RI i

    Towns of the Watershed iii

Table of Contents v

    Introduction 1

    Key to Map Symbols 4

Attleboro 5

    Bungay River Nature Preserve 7

    Dodgeville Pond 13

    Riverfront Park 19

    Balfour Park 23

    Larson Woods 27

    Lawrence Wildlife Preserve 31

    Oak Knoll Audubon 35

    Attleboro Springs Wildlife Refuge 39

    Lee's Pond 43

North Attleboro **45**

    Fish Hatchery 47

    WWI Memorial Park 51

    Barbara Road Beach/ Upper Falls Pond 55

    Martin Conservation Area/ Lower Falls Pond 59

    Chorney Property 63

    Whiting Pond 67

Plainville **69**

    Telford Park Trail 71

    Eagle Scout Nature Trail 75

    John Bowman Trail 79

Seekonk **83**

    Seekonk Meadows 85

    Gammino Pond Conservation Area 89

    Seacunke Sanctuary 95

    Newman Crossing 99

    Caratunk Wildlife Refuge 103

    Town Hall Runnins River Trail 107

    Edna Martin Wildlife Refuge 113

East Providence **117**

Hunt's Mills 119

Turner Reservoir 125

Bridgham Farm 131

Freedom Green-Boat Trip 135

East Bay Bike Path 141

Boyden Heights 149

Sabin Point 153

Crescent Park 157

Willett Pond 161

Jones Pond 165

Pawtucket 169

Ten Mile River Greenway 171

Reservation Trail 175

Slater Park 179

Slater Mill 183

Acknowledgments 187

Editor's Note 188

Introduction

As in the second edition of *Easy Walks in Massachusetts*, and *More Easy Walks in Massachusetts*, the focus of this book is on easy walking trails, with additional paddling excursions included. This edition covers the six towns that host the Ten Mile River watershed: Attleboro, North Attleboro, Plainville, Seekonk, East Providence, and Pawtucket. This third volume in the series offers yet more walking trails, with river access points as well.

Names or initials are included in ( ) at the end of each chapter. This indicates the author(s) of each entry, photo credit, and/or those who provided substantial support for confirming important details for access. Some entries in the book offer opportunities for kayaking and canoeing, many welcome dogs, and others accommodate horseback riding; a few also permit mountain biking. Several trails are handicapped-accessible. Some are newly developed. Trails in the planning phase were not included.

Many trails listed here are relatively short—one to two miles on average—and most are well maintained. Many are wide enough to allow for friends or families to walk together side by side. Several properties have additional connecting trails for those who are interested in longer, more challenging walks.

Maps to trail heads are provided, but these are neither trail maps nor do they accurately indicate property boundaries. We recommend downloading detailed trail maps (when available) using search terms indicated in the trail listings. Our hope is that the reader will better understand how to find trail heads and will see where some are connected or quite near others included in this book. Plan to visit additional trails that are nearby—sometimes they are right around the corner.

Trail access and trail conditions may change over time, and rights of access (parking, trail routes) cannot always be guaranteed. Avoid blocking roads, gates, or access points with cars or other vehicles. "People trails" have appeared over time and these may not honor known town or property lines. It's important to respect all posted and private properties.

Use common sense while outdoors. Wear comfortable, closed-toe shoes to protect your feet. Bring water, preferably in a light backpack that leaves your hands free. Hats are helpful. Windbreakers and/or raincoats can make the difference between a fun walk and a miserable one. Dress in layers.

Most hikes listed here are relatively easy—hence the book series' titles! But be aware that falls, tripping hazards, slippery wet rocks, and other accidents are always possible.

Learn to recognize poison ivy, which is ubiquitous in the eastern U.S. The hairy roots of poison ivy, sometimes quite large, can climb many trees, and they are as poisonous as the plant's foliage. Winter is no protection, so do use caution. Technu and Zanfel brand topical lotions are helpful in preventing or mitigating the worst effects of this plant.

Ticks are a concern in almost any weather, but especially in spring and after a rain. Light-colored clothing can help to spot these disease vectors. Tuck your long pants into your boots or socks to discourage ticks; but be aware, also, that tiny nymph-stage ticks can enter your socks between the weave. "Tick checks" at the end of hikes are a good practice.

Fall is hunting season in New England. State properties often allow hunting in season. Mass Audubon properties *never* allow hunting. Dress both yourself and your dogs, if they're with you, in blaze orange; the more the better!

Always let someone know where you are going. Cell phones often have little or no reception in the woods, especially in hilly areas, so do not depend on them for seeking help.

Try to avoid taking walks close to dusk. The sun sets quickly in winter, and a darkened, unfamiliar trail is a perfect opportunity for injury. Carry a flashlight—or better still, a headlamp—in your pack, just in case. Don't treat the outdoors as a place where "carefree" means "careless." Most important, get outside and have fun!

Key to Map Symbols

wheelchair accessible

restrooms

horseback riding permitted

no dogs allowed

paved bicycle trail

canoe access

dogs on leash

unimproved bike trail

swimming beach

numbered road

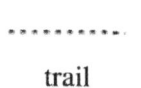

trail

fishing

approx. property boundary

parking

surface waters

Attleboro

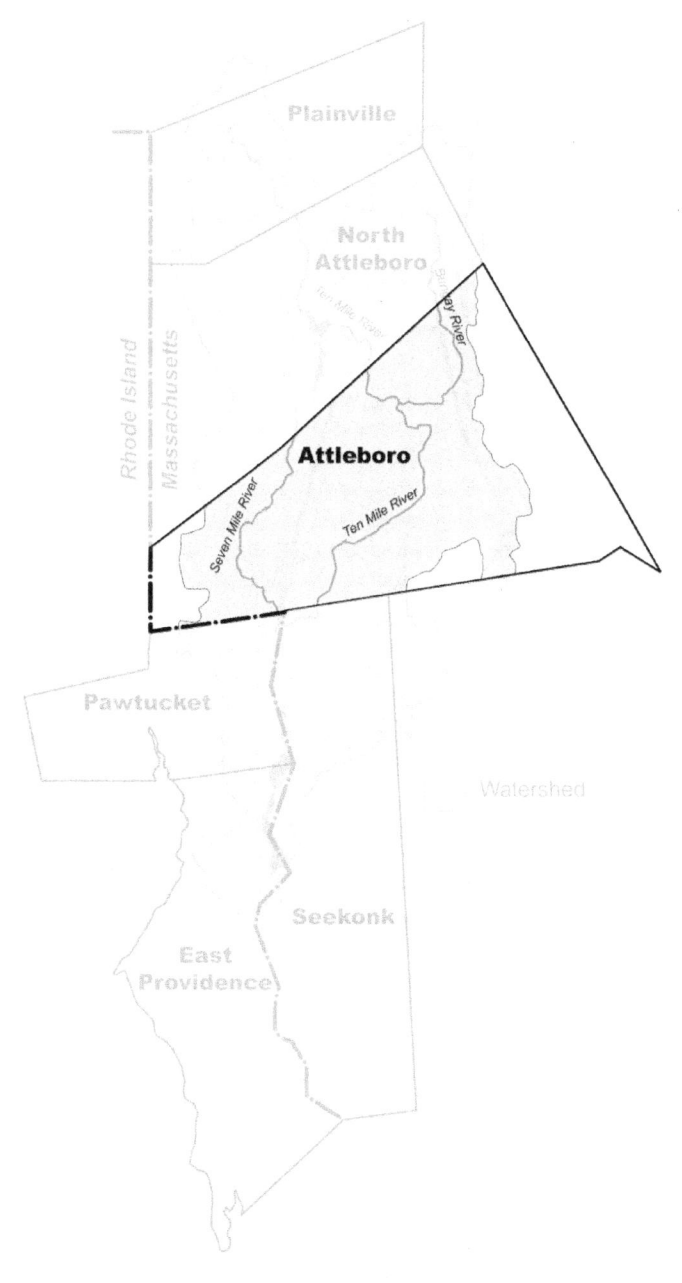

ATTLEBORO

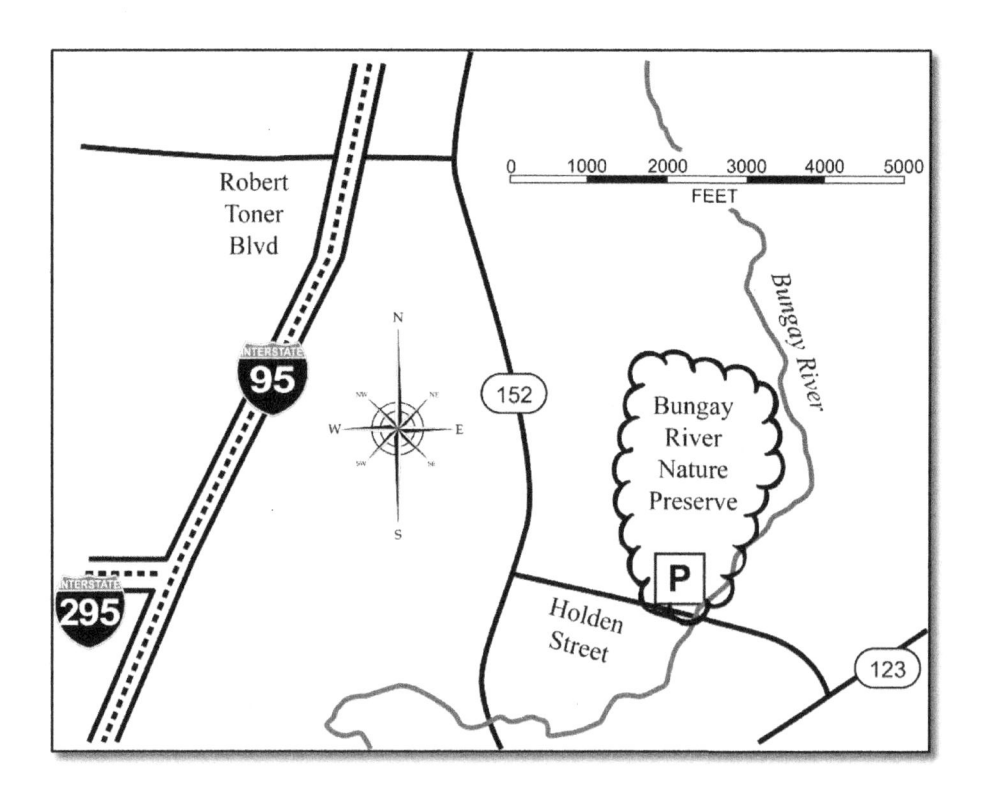

Bungay River Nature Preserve

Features: Canoe put-in, river access, trail alongside the river.

Trail Map: N/A

GPS Coordinates: 41°57'13.37"N 71°16'49.70"W

Directions: Holden Street, Attleboro. From Attleboro center follow Rt.152 north 0.75 miles to Holden St. and turn right at the large green "Holden Street" sign. From North Attleboro and exit 5 (Robert Toner Blvd) Rt.95, follow Rt.152 south for 1 mile and turn left on to Holden St. at the large green "Holden Street" sign. Follow Holden

St. for about 0.4 mile to the parking lot on the left where there is a dip in the road.

Cost: Free.

Bathrooms: Not available.

Best time to visit: Walking, year round. Canoeing, spring summer, fall.

Trail Conditions: Most of the river upstream is too narrow for more than one canoe. Newly blazed trail is packed dirt.

Distance: Up to 2 miles paddling north. Trail (accessed from parking area, opposite from canoe launch), is about 0.3 miles in length, out to power lines.

Parking: Free, for up to 8 cars, directly off Holden St.

The Bungay River is a little known tributary of the Ten Mile River whose headwaters are in Plainville, Mass. The Bungay is a small stream which is generally not navigable. It joins the Ten Mile River in nearby Attleboro center near the Colonel Blackinton Inn.

In addition to the canoe launch area, the Boy Scouts have created a newly-blazed trail from the parking area alongside the river. The Attleboro Land Trust (ALT) manages about 270 acres of these wetlands known as the Bungay River Nature Preserve. Trail head access is at the opposite end of the parking area from the canoe launch. The trail is short, but travels through woodland in which you'll find stone walls, possible vernal pools, and swampy areas. The trail markers end at the power lines. Possible additional hiking is available following the power lines.

The Bungay can be described in two words as a pleasant float at most any time of year. Others have described it as the best red maple swamp trip in the state of Massachusetts. Access to the river is easily gained at the canoe launch off Holden Street. The river is about 25' wide at this point and your view upstream is unobstructed for several hundred feet. Soon you will enter some shorter passages and forget that you have left the city. We have usually paddled on the river in the spring and there is virtually no current that you can detect whether you are paddling up or downstream. While on the river it seemed as if I was in a green orb drifting through a lush, green rainforest being pushed onward by a gentle breeze. I have never seen the river too low to travel. There is little shore access in most places as the banks are too overgrown.

As you paddle slowly upstream, the waterway narrows. In about two miles you will have to duck and push small branches out of your way to continue upstream. Use your best judgment for when to turn around, depending on water depth and how your canoe or kayak is handling. Along the way there is a lunch spot which is difficult for more than two boats to find and land in the vegetation. Here there is a small pine grove with a path to some gravel banks and power lines.

You will see some wildlife along the river depending on which season you travel. When we visited in mid-May we were escorted upstream by red winged blackbirds at every turn of the river and easily heard their high pitched screech. A flock of Canada geese tried to keep their distance from us by swimming upstream and soon gave up and flew off. Yellow speckled sun turtles warily watched our approach before finally diving into the water in groups of four or more.

The Bungay River is being evaluated for a designated Wild and Scenic status as one segment of the Ten Mile River watershed. It is a jewel which must be preserved. (Bill Luther, MTH)

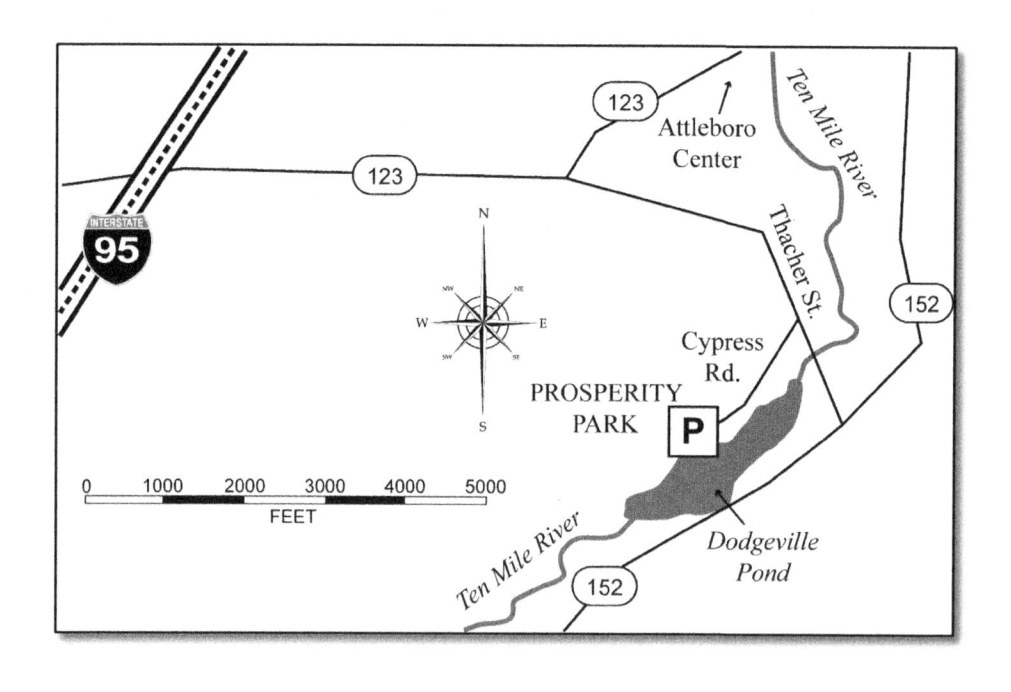

ATTLEBORO

Dodgeville Pond

Features: Canoe put-in, historic cemetery, former cotton mill.

Trail Map: N/A

GPS Coordinates: 41°55'31.27"N 71°17'36.25"W

Directions: Prosperity Park. From Attleboro center, South Main St, Rt.152, travel 1.3 miles south to right onto Thacher St. in Attleboro, or from the intersection of Rt.95 and the end of Rt.295 in Attleboro, travel south on Rt.95 to the next exit, Rt.123 and head east 1.5 miles on Rt.123 to right onto Thacher St. to Cypress St. on your right.

Drive 0.2 miles, Prosperity Park is on your left at the end of Cypress Street.

Cost: Free.

Bathrooms: None available.

Best Time to Visit: Late spring, early fall.

Trail Conditions: Easy paddling, landing option to walk in Dodge family cemetery area.

Distance: 20-acre pond with landing and cemetery, 2 miles round trip, including Thacher Brook.

Parking: Up to 5 cars on Cypress Street.

Dodgeville Pond in Attleboro was created by the impoundment of the Ten Mile River in the 19th century, next to a former cotton mill on South Main St. The former mill building, which originally dates back to 1812, is now a construction storage facility. You will want to stay away from the southwest side of the pond. Amtrak trains roar by at high speeds. You should not land to investigate. Passage downstream would be difficult due to private property crossings.

On the opposite bank from the canoe launch at Prosperity Park, the shore juts out and has a landing where the ground rises slightly. Here you will find the hidden cemetery of the Dodge family, whose history underlies the development of the mill and village which arose on the banks of the river. This cotton mill thrived through the 19th century before finally closing its doors in 1984. The mill is of historical significance to the area.

In the cemetery you will find a 20-foot tall magnificent obelisk gravemarker where John Crawford Dodge, the father of the Dodgeville Mill Dodge family, is buried. The grave is inscribed with the tribute "To our Father." He lived from 1798 to 1856. Farther downstream you will find the Hebronville Mill and village, which has a similar history.

Once you have finished your tour of the family cemetery, continue paddling upstream to the inlet and Thacher Street. When I paddled this pond in September there was a mat of invasive plants which I had to paddle-plow through. The plants were thick for about 25 feet before I found the channel.

In a short distance I saw a sun turtle basking in the afternoon sun. Soon I found a small colony of birds. Canada geese and mallards all made a racket, splashed, and flew off as I paddled closer, somewhat perturbed at my intrusion. On the side of the river I saw several great blue herons and as I approached they quietly flapped and flew off. I saw no people until I crossed under the Thacher St. bridge, where fishermen were casting off, hoping to catch a few largemouth bass before throwing them back in.

Here the river valley is wide and attractive. Maple trees are abundant and you would not realize that this river was once badly polluted by nearby factories. Thacher Brook enters on your right in a wide delta with short-growth bushes.

Our short, 2-mile paddle was completed in just over an hour's time. This was in September and it was windy. There is potential to continue upstream on a calm day, depending on the depth of the river and how fast the downstream current is at the time. In the summer the pond will be a little murky and muddy. In cooler months the water will appear to be very clean. Early fall and late spring would be the time to spend just paddling for fun. (Bill Luther)

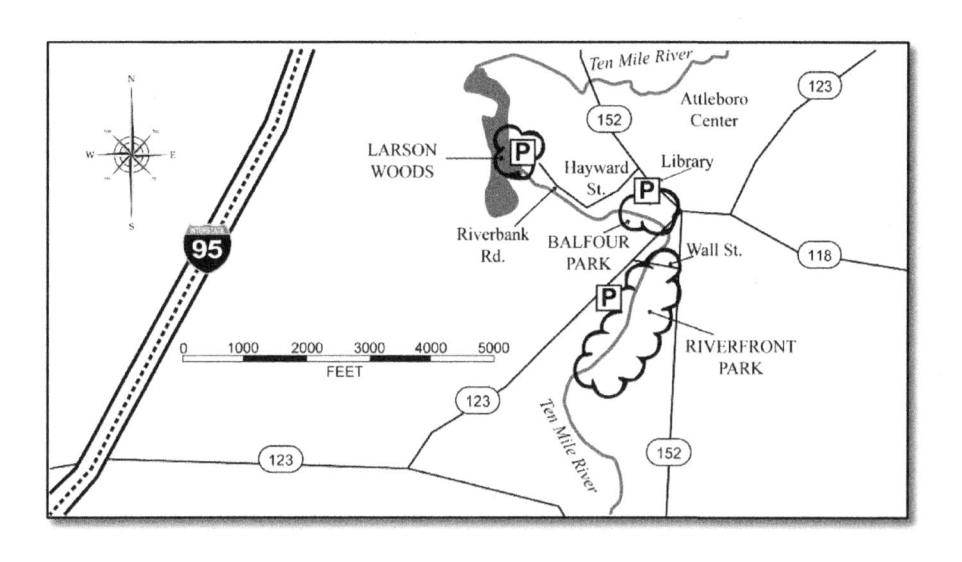

ATTLEBORO

Riverfront Park

Features: 0.25 mile paved rail trail alongside the Ten Mile River at edge of downtown Attleboro. Part of the Attleboro Linear Walkway through downtown Attleboro. Canoe launch into the Ten Mile River.

Trail Map: N/A

GPS Coordinates: 41°56'27.21"N 71°17'14.00"W

ATTLEBORO

Directions: Riverfront Dr. Travel on Rt.152 south of Attleboro center for 0.1 mile, turn right onto Wall Street, first left is Riverfront Drive, park is directly across from commuter rail station.

Cost: Free.

Bathrooms: Porta-potties seasonally.

Best time to visit: Year Round.

Trail conditions: Paved railtrail.

Distance: 0.25 mile. Additional mileage possible when combined with travel to Balfour Park, Larson Woods, which makes the Attleboro Linear Walkway, about 2 miles total, round trip.

Parking: On street designated parking (2-hour limit) alongside the park the entire length of the trail.

Attleboro recently opened a new park alongside the banks of the Ten Mile River, transforming a bleak industrial strip of land into an appealing spot just south of downtown. The new park, dedicated to the former mayor, Judith Robbins, offers a short, quarter mile bike path/walking path that is flanked by grass and perennial gardens. Several picnic tables and benches are available.

Riverfront Park was the brainchild of former Mayor Judith Robbins who toiled on this project for ten years. The park was dedicated in her name in July of 2017. She secured over 6 million dollars of funding to move DPW sheds and facilities to another location, buy property, get environmental clearance on the grounds overlooking the river, and provide landscaping. She had a vision to create an urban village, and to establish green belts along dilapidated sections of the city.

The actual Riverfront Park is a relatively short walk which parallels the river along a landscaped front. The park has a feeling of being artificially created and, indeed, it was recently altered. Invasive plants have been removed. On your visit, enjoy a clear unobstructed view of the river. This is an urban walkway. The banks of the river have been virtually cleared of litter. The river moves quickly in this stretch.

The walkway is very well lit at night. (Ernie Germani, Bill Luther, Keith Gonsalves, MTH).

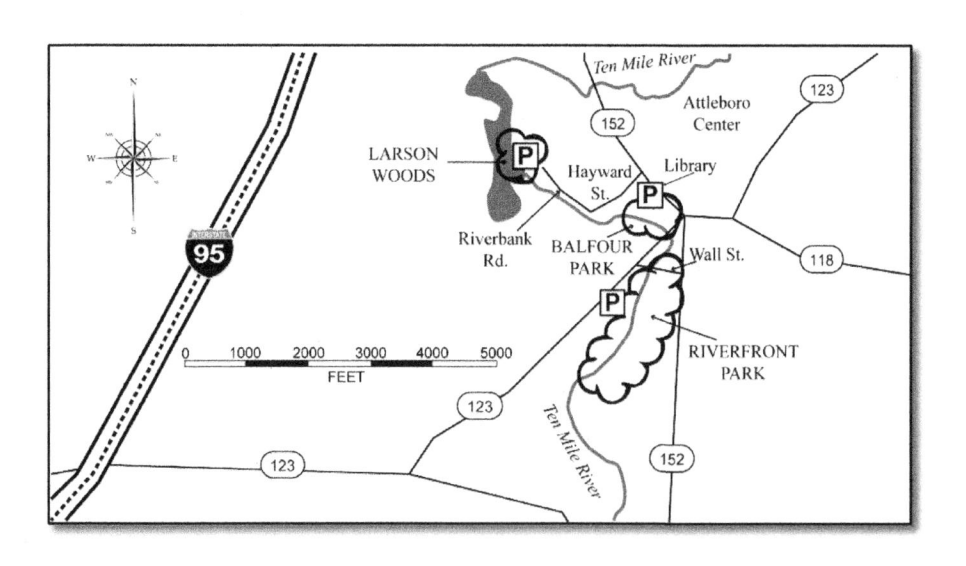

ATTLEBORO

Balfour Park

Features: Urban park next to Attleboro Library, skate park, ice skating rink in winter, volleyball net, Ten Mile River flows next to park.

Trail Map: N/A

GPS Coordinates: 41°56'38.39"N 71°17'06.39"W

Directions: 74 North Main Street, near intersection of Rts. 152 and 123. Best access from municipal parking area next to Attleboro Public Library

ATTLEBORO

Cost: Free.

Bathrooms: At library when open.

Best time to visit: Open year round.

Trail conditions: Paved walkways.

Distance: Small park, walk can be extended by following the river to connecting parks, Larson Woods to the north and Riverfront Park to the south. About 2 miles round trip.

Parking: Municipal parking (for a small fee) next to Attleboro Library, which is adjacent to the park (on Rt.152) or at Community Gardens on Hayward Street.

Combine a walk through Balfour Park, Riverfront Park, and Larson Woodlands and finish the trip in a little over an hour's time. Attleboro was once a capital of the jewelry industry. The Balfour Company was a leading employer in the city especially in the production of specialty commemorative rings. The Balfour family owned and donated this small section of land along the Ten Mile River.

A footbridge in one corner of the park crosses the Ten Mile River over to Riverfront St. and connects to Larson Woods by road via the Community Gardens on Hayward St. The park itself is dedicated to recreation with a skateboard park, volleyball court, ice rink, and children's playground facilities.

Other features make the park a wonderful place just to explore.

ATTLEBORO

The city has kept it clean and attractive. It is not well lit at night and you should use caution if you walk after dusk. (Bill Luther, MTH)

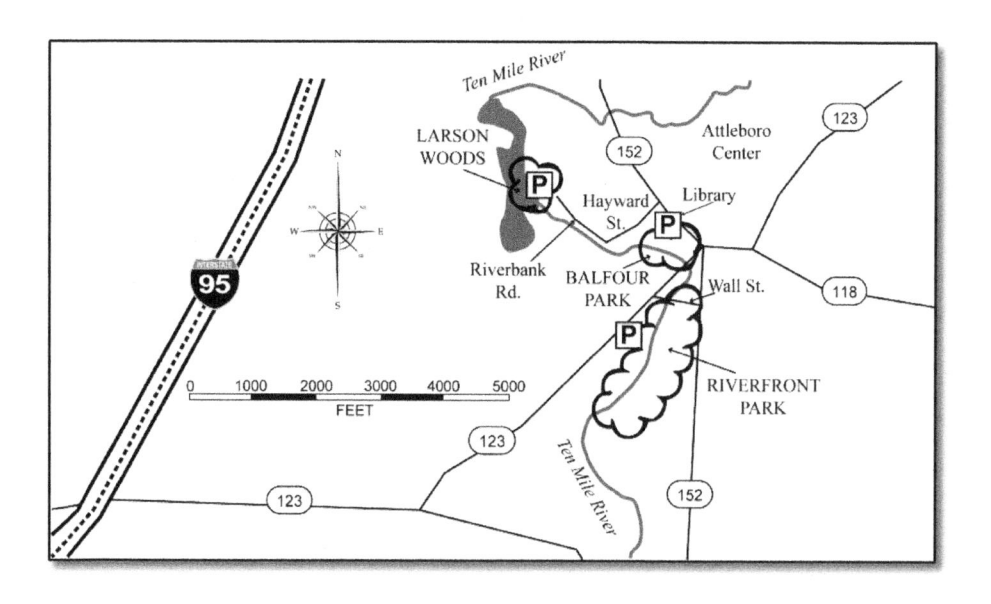

ATTLEBORO

ATTLEBORO

Larson Woods

Features: River views, small canoe launch area where the Bungay and Ten Mile River meet at Mechanic's Pond.

Trail Map: N/A

GPS Coordinates: 41°56'45.82"N 71°17'32.65"W

Directions: Riverbank Rd. Southbound, from Rt.152 just before the Attleboro Library in Attleboro center, turn right onto Hayward St.

ATTLEBORO

drive 0.2 miles to right onto Riverbank Rd. (at Community Gardens). Larson Woods is 0.1 miles up on Riverbank Rd. Northbound on Rt.152, from Attleboro Center, 0.2 miles past intersections with Rts. 123 and 118, turn left just past the Library onto Hayward St. At Community Gardens, bear right onto Riverbank Rd., travel 0.1 mile to Larson Woods, directly across from Thomas Willet School.

Cost: Free.

Bathrooms: Not available.

Best time to visit: Year Round.

Trail conditions: Packed dirt trail to river.

Distance: 0.25 mile.

Parking: On street parking, or parking at Community Gardens on Hayward Street.

Larson Woods is a four-acre conservation area administered by the Attleboro Land Trust (ALT). It borders the Ten Mile River and Bungay River and is just a short hike from the city center. The woodland offers a kiosk, with several trails that travel through the woods to the confluence of the Bungay and Ten Mile Rivers. The land was donated by longtime resident Ray Larson and acquired in 1997 by ALT and dedicated in 1999.

Larson Woods offers a great view of the river. If you walk straight back into these woods from the kiosk you will see the river below from a height of land and see a lower trail just another 20 feet below. Head down to the river, or keep walking to your right for another 150 feet and come to a spot where the Bungay and Ten Mile rivers come together to form Mechanic's Pond. This is a pretty spot called Sandy Point, which is the backwater above the Mechanics Falls dam. There is a remote, natural feeling to the area.

Riverbank Rd. follows the river for another 500 feet back toward the Community Gardens and Balfour Park, which allows for a walk alongside the river on a graveled path the entire way. For the adventurous who want to visit four city parks you could continue to Community Gardens, Balfour Park, and Riverfront Park. Community Gardens is at the corner of Hayward and Riverbank Roads. If you connected all four parks by walking, you will cover about 1 mile one way and log about 2 total miles with your return trip. The gardens have existed since 1998. All spots at the community garden are currently claimed. (Ernie Germani, MTH)

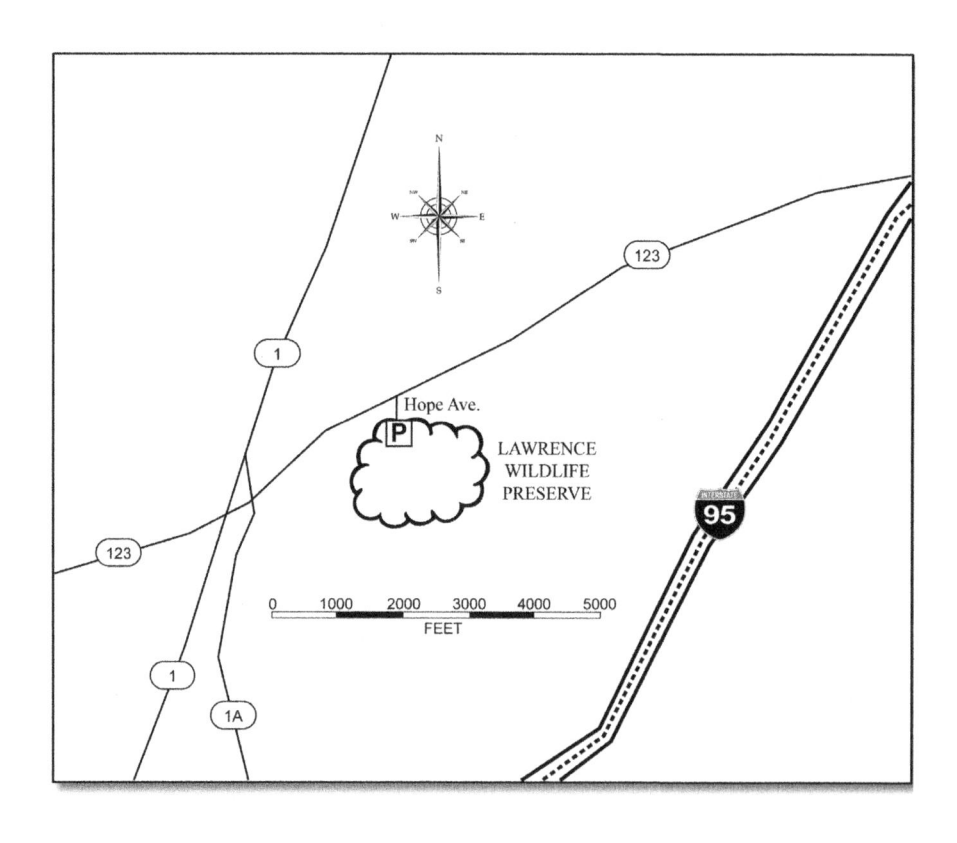

ATTLEBORO

ATTLEBORO

Lawrence Wildlife Preserve

Features: Seven Mile River flows through 53-acre property.

Trail Map: Search "Attleboro Land Trust Lawrence wildlife refuge"

GPS Coordinates: 41°55'23.21N 71°20'56.47"W

Directions: 99 Hope Ave. (NOT Hope St.!)

From the north end of Rt.295 at Rt.95, travel south on Rt.95 for 1.5 miles to the Rt.123 exit. Head west on Rt.123 for 1.6 miles, Hope Ave. is on your left. Or from Attleboro Center, Follow Rt.123 for

ATTLEBORO

3.75 miles to Hope Ave., which is directly across from the American Legion Hall. Go to end of Hope Ave., about 3 blocks.

Cost: None.

Bathrooms: Not available.

Best Time to Visit: Year Round.

Trail Conditions: Undeveloped, limited trails.

Distance: 0.3 miles.

Parking: Space for only one car presently.

The wooden sign post indicates that you have found an Attleboro Land Trust (ALT) location and the fact that the woods are straight ahead of you means you have arrived. Not many people come to explore this hidden jewel.

Anthony Lawrence donated 43 acres of land which became ALT property in 1994. Subsequent land donations have increased the total size to 53 acres. The Seven Mile River flows through this property and it is wonderful that they have protected the aquifer from development. Retail development on Rt.1, Washington St., extends for miles nearby. The Boy Scouts have cleared some trails but one of the loop trails is lacking blazed markings. The preserve is primitive, kept in a natural state. The actual hiking trails, some quite wide, do not extend far into the wetlands.

Tannery Brook flows through this property. The water was flowing fast and was quite wide. I thought about jumping over it but thought better of it and turned around.

The entire trip took me about 20 minutes and may have been 1.2 miles long. I enjoyed the short hike but hope that ALT may expand the trails so people can observe more wetlands. I saw many birds and would expect that many animals benefit from this protection. (Bill Luther, Ben Cote)

ATTLEBORO

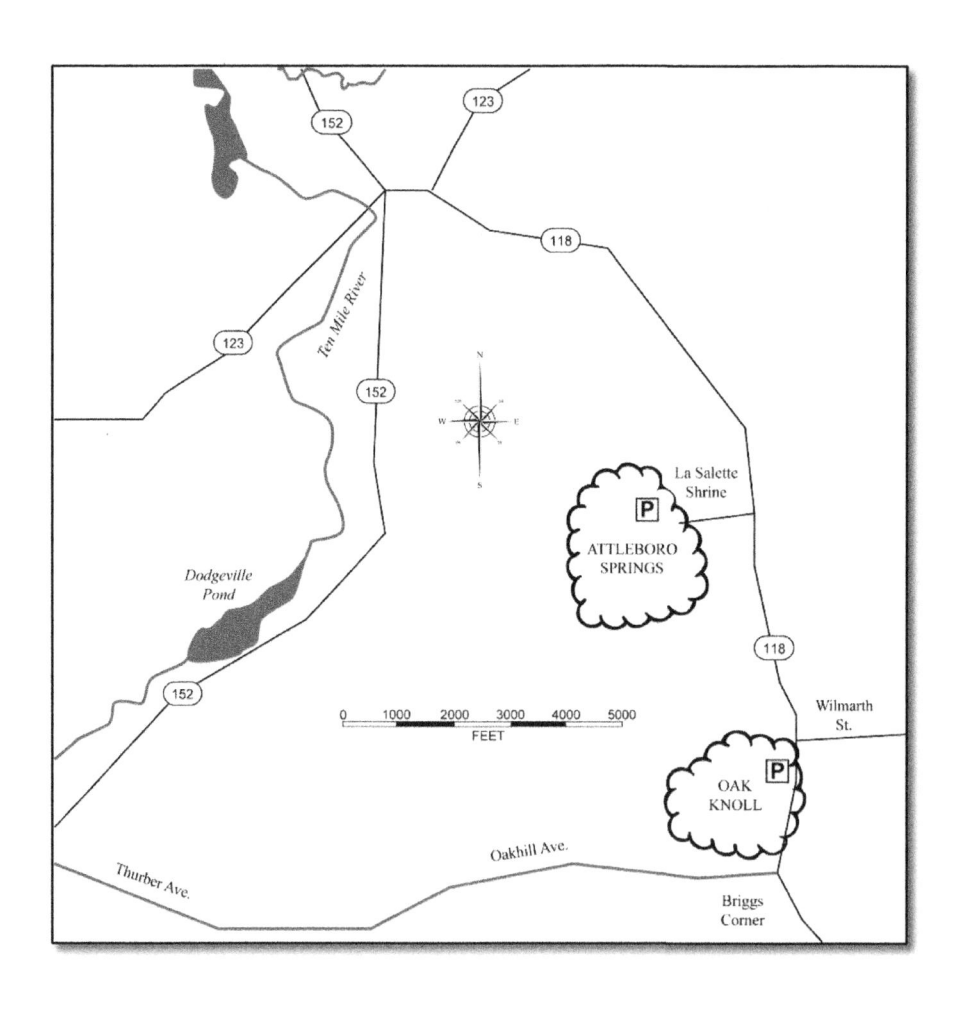

ATTLEBORO

Oak Knoll Audubon

Features: Audubon Property, loop trails around both pond and wetlands, water views.

Trail Map: Search "MA Audubon Oak Knoll" then "About," then "Trails"

GPS Coordinates: 41°54'53.68N 71°15'28.20"W

ATTLEBORO

Directions: 1417 Park Street, Rt.118. Take Rt.95 to exit 5 (Rt.152). Turn left off the exit ramp and take a right onto Rt.152 south. After 1.5 miles at the center of town, turn left onto Park Street (becomes Rt.118). Look for La Sallette signs. (Oak Knoll is not far past La Sallette Shrine). Follow Park Street for 2 miles; road will curve right.

Cost: Free to Audubon members, $2 suggested donation for non-members.

Bathrooms: Available when visitor's center is open. Sanctuary office closed on Mondays, but trails are open for visitors.

Best time to visit: Year round.

Trail conditions: Packed dirt track, clearly blazed. Boardwalks through wetlands areas allow for easy walking.

Distance: 51 acres, 1.5 miles of trail.

Parking: Large parking lot for at least 20 cars, open daily even when visitor's center is closed.

Oak Knoll is a Massachusetts Audubon Society property that offers about 1.5 miles of trails. There are two loops connected by the main trail. The first, the Puddingstone Loop, winds through an area of oaks and stone walls. The second loop wraps around the shores of Lake Talaquega, a haven for local birds including ducks and geese.

The lake in summer months tends to fill with lily pads. The main

ATTLEBORO

trail runs from the parking area back to the pond passing over Thacher Brook and through an area of swamp dominated by red maples. The main trail has several sections of boardwalk through the swampy areas. The property also offers a small meadow, a marsh, and a visitor's center. The trail on this property is marked, as are other Audubon properties, with blue dots for heading away from the visitor's center, yellow dots for returning to the parking area. (Bill Luther, Ernie Germani, Keith Gonsalves, MTH)

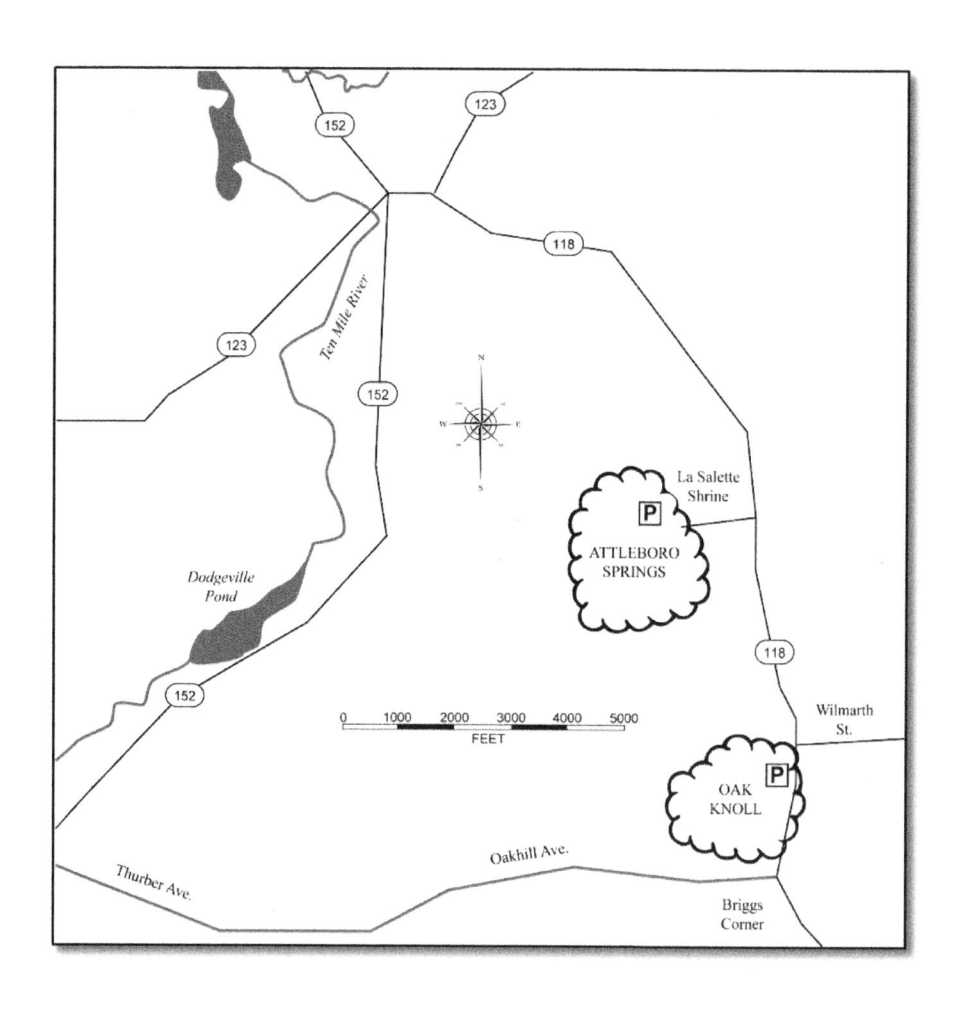

ATTLEBORO

ATTLEBORO

Attleboro Springs Wildlife Refuge

Features: Handicapped Accessible trail, open meadow, small pond.

Trail Map: Search: "MA Audubon Attleboro Springs"

GPS Coordinates: 41°55'42.38"N 71°15'54.50"W

Directions: 947 Park Street, Rt.118, at back of La Sallette Shrine. Take Rt.95 to exit 5 (Robert Toner Blvd.). Turn left off the exit ramp

ATTLEBORO

and take a right onto Rt.152 south. After 1.5 miles at Attleboro center,, turn left onto Park Street. Look for La Salette signs. Follow Park Street (which becomes Rt.118) for 1.5 miles; road will curve right. Pass the La Salette Shrine and take your next right at the stone gatehouse. The sanctuary is located at the end of the boulevard.

Cost: Free.

Bathrooms: No.

Best time to visit: Year round; parking is challenging during Christmas season (near dusk and into evening) because of proximity to the Shrine, a very popular seasonal attraction with Christmas lights.

Trail conditions: Trail around Brothers Pond is ADA accessible, packed stone dust with guide rope for the sight impaired, along with Braille signs. Piggery Path and Esker trail more challenging (some roots and rocks) but walkable.

Distance: 3 miles of trails.

Parking: Access parking from Rt.118 by road between two La Salette parking lots—take paved road between the two lots to the very back, parking is next to trail head.

Starting at a small parking area at the end of the middle entrance road to La Salette Shrine, the Reflection Trail is immediately ahead of you and is ADA accessible. The hard packed stone dust surface offers a rope guideline to circle Brothers Pond. Braille signposts are erected at intervals all along this trail, along with a guide rope to assist those with visual impairments.

The Oak Forest Trail, accessed from the Reflection Trail, gets quite narrow in places and can be buggy, rooty and rocky in spots, and is not easy walking, but a beautiful trail nonetheless. Those with mobility concerns will do best to avoid this path, while others will surely enjoy the walk.

From the Reflection Trail, head over to the meadow. Soon you will come across the trail that is marked with blue circles. Follow that to the Esker Loop. Then follow the yellow circle trail back to the Piggery Path which leads back again to the meadow. Both these paths are somewhat challenging, but with care can be navigated safely. (Ernie Germani, Keith Gonsalves, MTH)

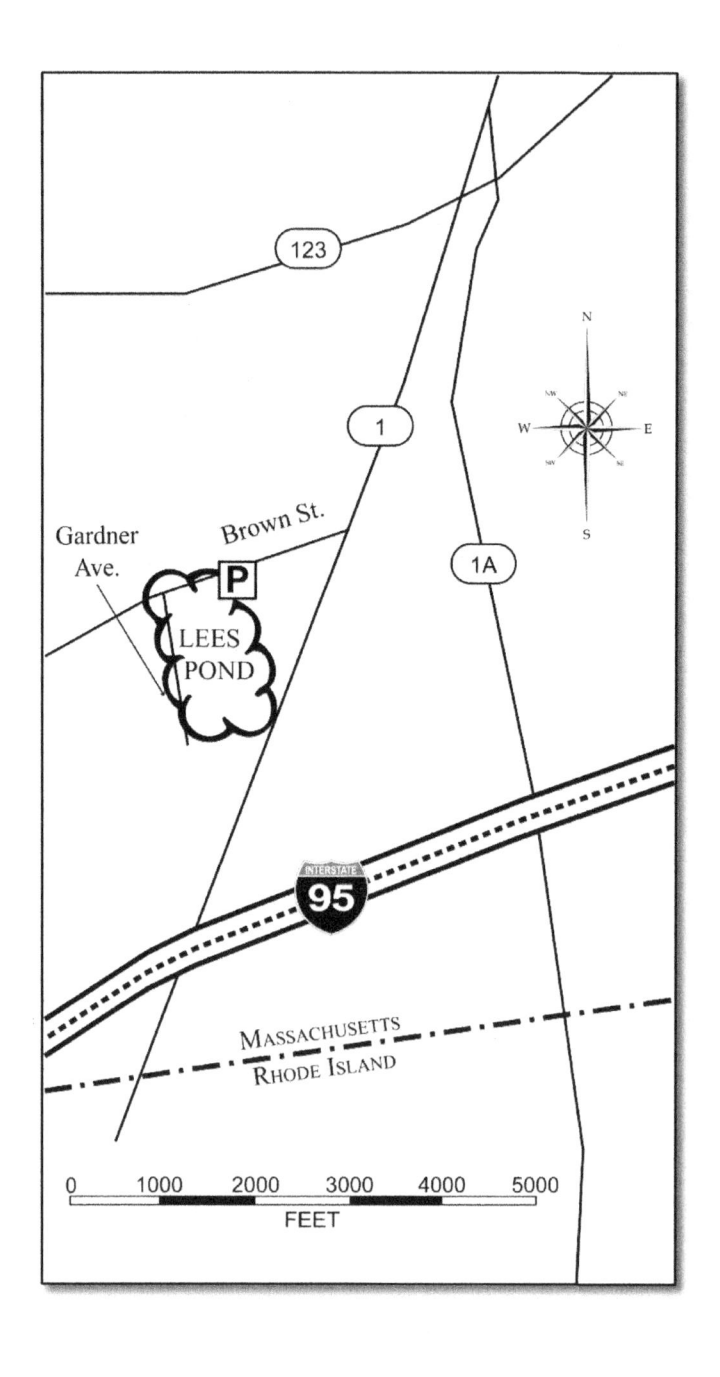

ATTLEBORO

ATTLEBORO

Lee's Pond

Features: Fitness Trail, water views, picnic area, swimming pool.

Trail Map: N/A

GPS Coordinates: 41°54'27.73"N 71°22'12.00"W

Directions: Gardner Ave. From the intersection of Rts.1 and 123 in South Attleboro, head south on Rt.1 for 0.75 mile to Brown Street, on the right. Gardner Ave. will be 0.5 mile on the left. Turn onto Gardner Ave., parking is almost immediately on your left.

ATTLEBORO

Cost: Free.

Bathrooms: Not Available.

Best time to visit: Year round.

Trail conditions: Asphalt/stone dust trail.

Distance: 0.75 mile fitness trail.

Parking: Space for at least 15 cars in designated parking areas next to park.

This small park nestled in a South Attleboro neighborhood offers a bit of everything. A 0.75 mile fitness trail follows the perimeter of the park. The trail is a combination of asphalt and stone dust.

Within the fitness trail is a skate park, basketball courts, playground, tot area, gazebo, football field, baseball fields, horseshoe and volleyball courts, picnic area, fish pond, war memorials, and a swimming pool. (Ernie Germani)

North Attleboro

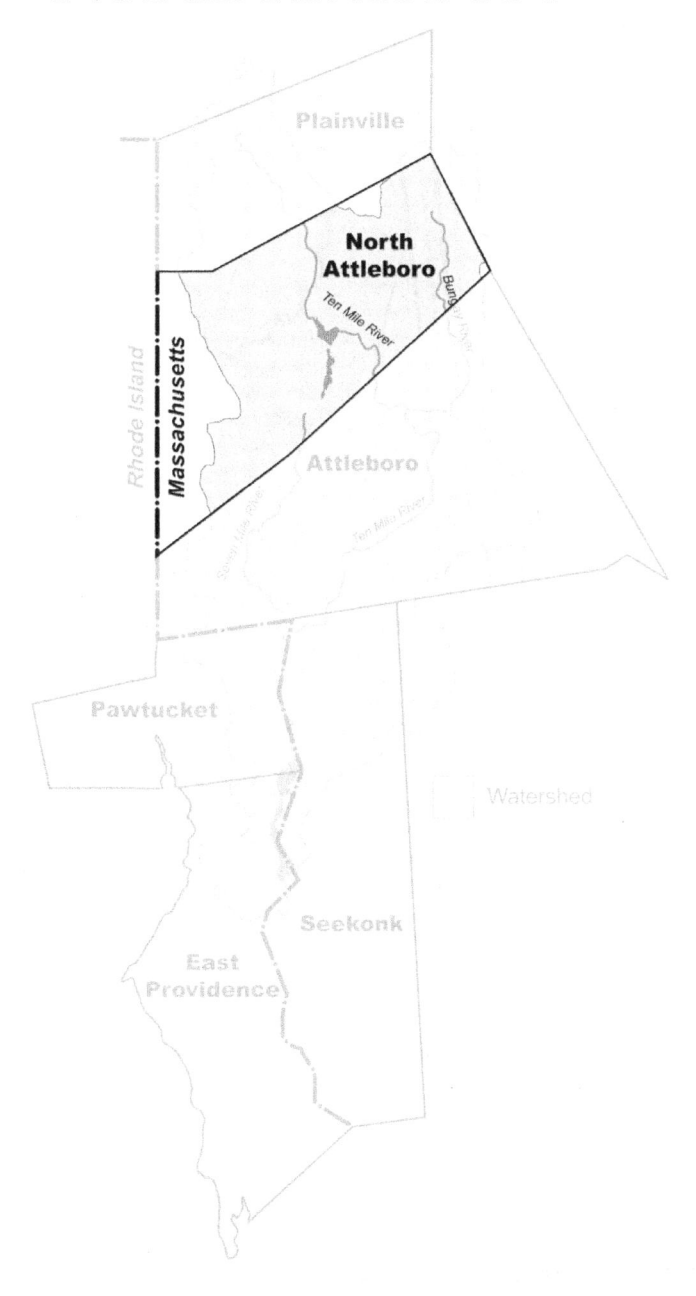

NORTH ATTLEBORO

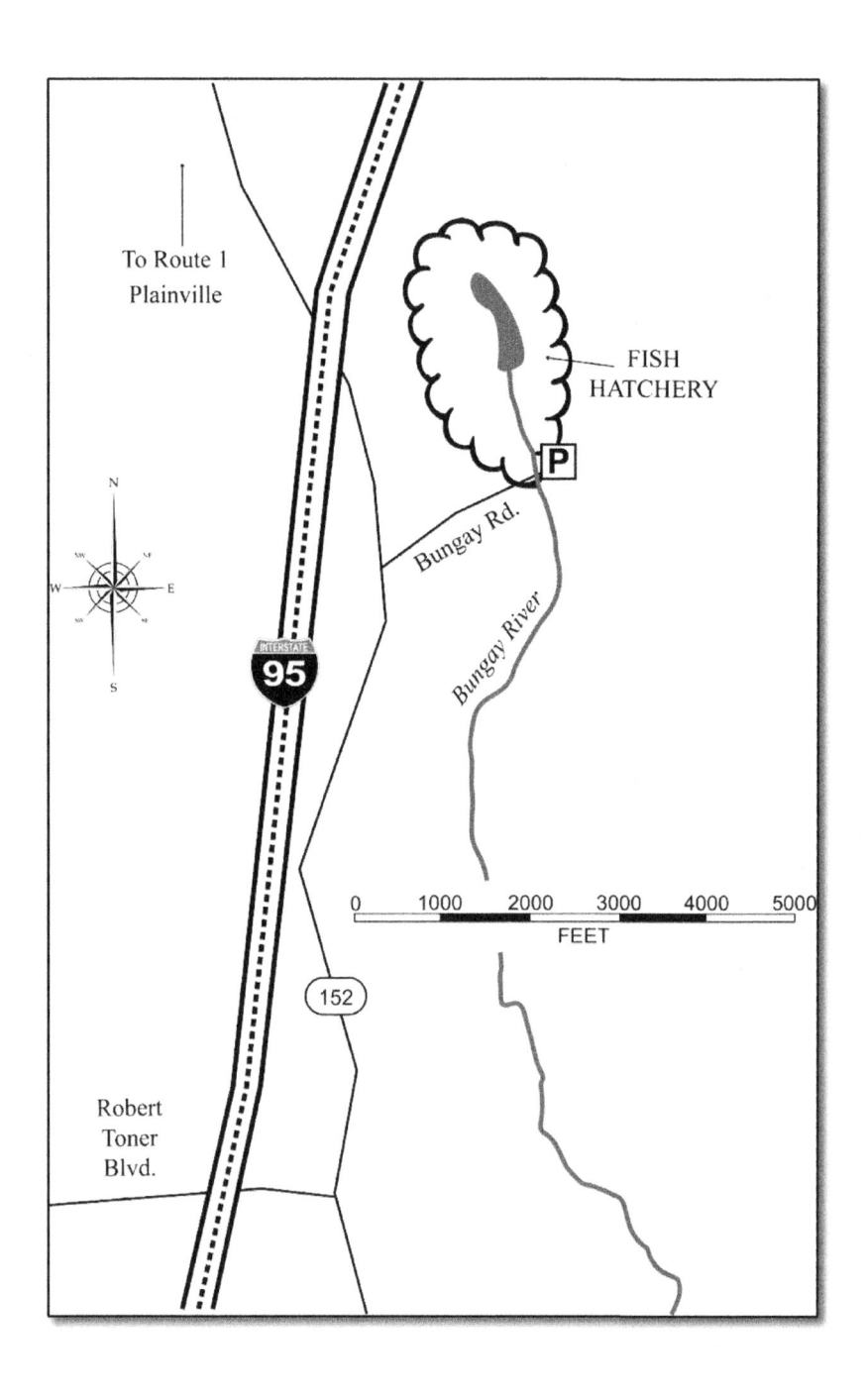

NORTH ATTLEBORO

Fish Hatchery

Features: Loop trail, water views, Bungay Brook, Story Walk®, U.S. Fish & Wildlife Fish Hatchery, tours of fish hatchery available.

Trail Map: Search: "North Attleboro Fish Hatchery"

NORTH ATTLEBORO

GPS Coordinates: 41°59'33.23"N 71°16'59.61"W

Directions: 144 Bungay Rd. From Rt.495 to Rt.1 south for 0.5 miles, second left onto Rt.152, follow for 3 miles to Bungay Rd. on the left. Fish Hatchery 0.4 miles down on the left.

Cost: Free.

Bathrooms: Yes, in headquarters building. Ring bell at front door.

Best Time to Visit: Open year round, 8 a.m.–3:45 p.m., closed Sundays and federal holidays.

Trail Conditions: Clear, marked, hard-packed dirt track. Some stairs with railings (do not meet ADA standards).

Distance: Loop trail is 0.8 miles.

Parking: Ample parking in front of headquarters building. Trail head is to the right, beyond headquarters building.

While the U.S Fish & Wildlife Service's North Attleboro Fish Hatchery's main purpose is raising fish for catch and release into New England streams and ponds, this is a great spot for spending time enjoying their 235 acre property. A marked trail provides an easy loop walk around the pond that is next to the hatchery, with a small bridge that takes visitors from one side of Bungay Brook to the other.

Additional unmarked, but cleared trails are available for the more energetic hiker. All these trails are wide enough to allow for at least two people to walk side by side.

We have seen plenty of birds on our walks—great blue herons perch in the dammed pond, ducks, and other woodland bird species frequent the area.

Make time to get a tour of the fish hatchery itself when you visit. (You may need to make an appointment for a tour—check their website.) The staff is friendly, helpful, and eager to share information about their work. Volunteers are often at work making this special place even better for visitors. (MTH)

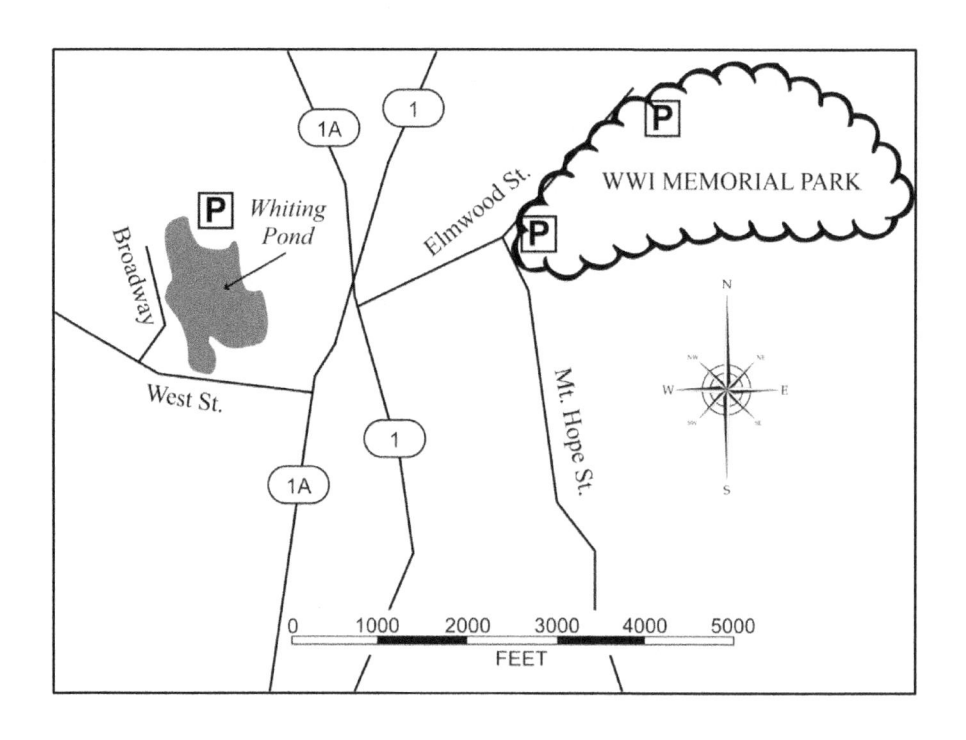

NORTH ATTLEBORO

NORTH ATTLEBORO

WWI Memorial Park

Features: Multiple marked loop trails, zoo, picnicking areas, view, sledding in winter.

Trail Map: Search: "North Attleboro park and recreation department"

GPS Coordinates: 42°00'04.89"N 71°18'59.50"W

Directions: 365 Elmwood Street. Rt.1 to Rt.106 eastbound for 1 mile to George Street on the right. 0.1 mile to right onto

NORTH ATTLEBORO

Messenger/Elmwood Street, travel 0.5 miles to park entrance, on left. OR Continue south of Rt.1 for 2.5 miles past Rt.106 to Elmwood Street, turn left at light onto Elmwood, travel 0.9 miles to park entrance, on right (just past North Attleboro Hockomock YMCA).

Cost: Free.

Bathrooms: Port-a-potties available throughout the park.

Best time to visit: Open year round, picnic reservations advised in summer.

Trail conditions: Clearly marked trails, paved circular path through park. Woodland trails are challenging, with rocks, roots, narrow, mostly of hard-packed dirt, a few wooden boardwalks through swampy areas.

Distance: Loop trails of 1 mile and some longer distances—check map, available on town recreation website.

Parking: Free, multiple parking areas.

The WWI Memorial Park in North Attleboro has a lot to offer—the zoo has been greatly improved from less optimal conditions in the past. Multiple walking trails offer easy walks as well as more challenging terrain, and these trails are used by many residents and visitors.

Recent renovations as well as strategic tree cutting has allowed for great views again at Lookout Point, something older residents recall. Until recently the view had been obscured by tree growth. Enjoy the whimsical gazebo that opens up to "the view," directly across from the zoo area.

In winter this is a popular spot for sledding. One or two power lines in the midst of the hill offer a challenge, but regardless, plenty of families flock to the park each snowfall to enjoy the ride, directly next to one of the parking areas. (MTH)

NORTH ATTLEBORO

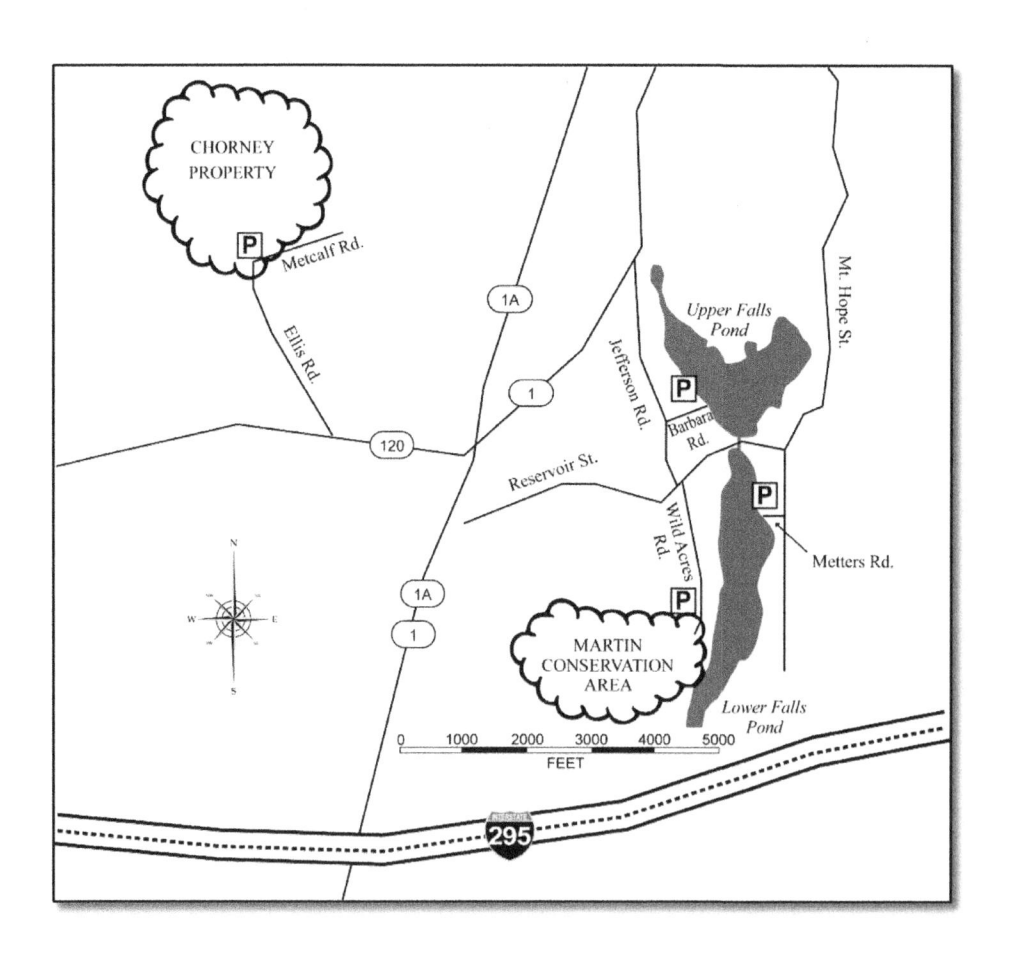

Barbara Road Beach/ Upper Falls Pond

Features: Swimming, canoeing, very short walking trail alongside pond. Boat launch for larger boats (for fee).

Trail Map: N/A

GPS Coordinates: 41°58'07.33"N 71°19'35.55"W

Directions: Barbara Rd. From intersection of Rt.1, Rt.120, and Rt.1A, head north on Rt.1 for 0.7 miles to right turn onto Rodney St.

NORTH ATTLEBORO

Go 0.1 mile to a right onto Jefferson St. Follow Jefferson 0.2 miles to a left onto Barbara Rd., which dead ends at parking area for beach.

Cost: $5 for MA residents, $20 for non MA residents.

Bathrooms: Seasonally available.

Best Time to Visit: 7 a.m. to Dusk, April to October. Gates closed at sunset, closed for the seas from November to March.

Trail Conditions: Motor boats permitted in pond, spring and fall will offer quieter conditions for kayaks and canoes.

Distance: Boat launch, bathing beach, very short walk along the shoreline from beach area.

Parking: Large parking area, charge for parking.

Barbara Beach is on Upper Falls Pond, a small comma-sized lake which exists because of a dam impoundment of the Ten Mile River.

The beach boating access here is small and is run by the North Attleboro Conservation Commission. A large grant improved this public beach in 2013. A lifeguard is on duty in summer and non-residents must pay a fee during the season. In October there were no attendants. No restroom facilities were available during my visit in the fall. Dogs are not allowed on the beach in the summer months. The park closes at 8:00 p.m. daily.

Multiple homes surround this 60-acre lake. I encountered a

motorboat taking out in October. The beach has a parking area for many trucks and trailers to drop off motorboats. Jet skies are not allowed. The average depth of Upper Falls is 20 feet with a maximum of 30 feet in depth.

I launched from the actual paved boat launch and paddled toward Lower Falls which connects to Upper thru a small culvert. A road separates the two bodies of water. In the southern corner I found a dam.

Just north of the beach and in one of the cove's corners was a small, walled stream near some apartments on the river bank. I paddled under a low bridge and went about 200 feet upstream and hit bottom, so I turned back. I had paddled a little over a mile and spent less than an hour on the water.

Upper Falls Pond is not a wilderness experience. I would paddle here after sunrise or before sunset. This will offer a nice, short, afternoon paddle during the cool season. Motorized boats frequent this area in summer months. (Bill Luther, MTH)

NORTH ATTLEBORO

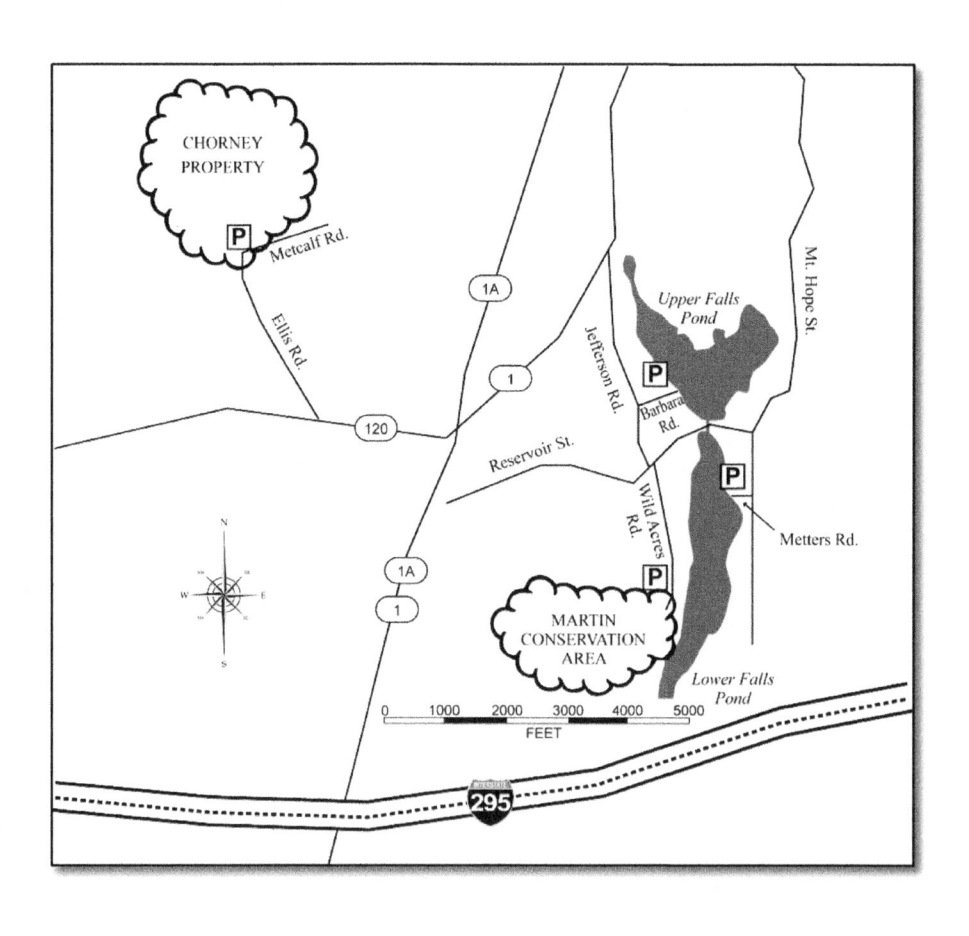

NORTH ATTLEBORO
Martin Conservation Area/ Lower Falls Pond

Features: Wetlands, limited trails, views of Lower Pond Falls, public boat ramp, canoeing.

Trail Map: N/A

GPS Coordinates: 41°57'30.44"N 71°19'33.48"W

Directions: To wooded preserve: From intersection of Rts. 120, 1, and 1A, travel 0.5 miles north on Rt.1 to right onto Rodney St. Go 0.1 mile to Jefferson St., turn right. Travel 0.5 miles to Reservoir St., turn left. Next right is Wild Acres Rd. (gravel road). Two boulders block road. To boat ramp at Lower Falls pond: Metters St. Same directions as above, but continue on Reservoir St. over dam, (0.3

miles) turn right onto Mt. Hope St., travel 0.2 mile to Metters St., on the right.

Cost: Free.

Bathrooms: Not available.

Best Time to Visit: Year round.

Trail Conditions: Unimproved dirt trails along shoreline, unmarked.

Distance: Under two miles of trail.

Parking: No designated parking.

The Martin Conservation area is located along the western shore of Lower Pond Falls. It is owned by the North Attleboro Conservation Commission. There are no signs or kiosk here indicating that you have entered public land. Hunting is permitted in season. On the opposite shore from Martin is a public boat ramp at the end of Metters St.

This area does not have blazed trails. The path is probably obvious, however, if you follow the shoreline. That would make a short 0.5 to 0.75 mile long walk. The area around the lake is wild and attractive without houses.

I noticed the remoteness of this lake. Homes are along the eastern shoreline, while the western shoreline is wooded and natural. No motorized boats are allowed in this area, only kayaks and canoes. Fishermen have told me that the trout fishing here is decent since the pond is stocked spring and fall. Lower Falls connects with the Upper

NORTH ATTLEBORO

Falls Pond and is actually the Ten Mile River by another name.

Once I reached the water I walked the shoreline to another open area that seemed well used. The path was well trampled and you could easily pick a route through. I did not see any blazes to mark the trail.

I noticed asphalt underfoot in one area. This must have been an old road abandoned years before when the lake was a local destination. I followed the road for over 0.5 mile as it approached Rt.295. The abandoned road continued but I turned around here as the trail veered off in a different direction.

No signs inform visitors how large the conservation area is or its boundaries. On a return trip I again followed the path next to the lake and looked to see if there were any obvious trails I had missed. On my way back to the car I scouted along the edges of the entry road. I did find one obscure trail which may have been the 1.5 mile trail that the area description I'd read had covered. If you park at the two boulders and walk until you can see the second fence enclosure, you would look to your right and see a cleared parking area which extends back about 75 feet to a lone oak tree on the edges. Walk behind the tree and you will pick up a visibly trampled path. It is not marked. It extends away from the lake and heads west toward Rt.1. Within the property are a small brook and pine groves. After heavy rains the swampy areas make many of these trails impassable. (Bill Luther, Ernie Germani, MTH)

NORTH ATTLEBORO

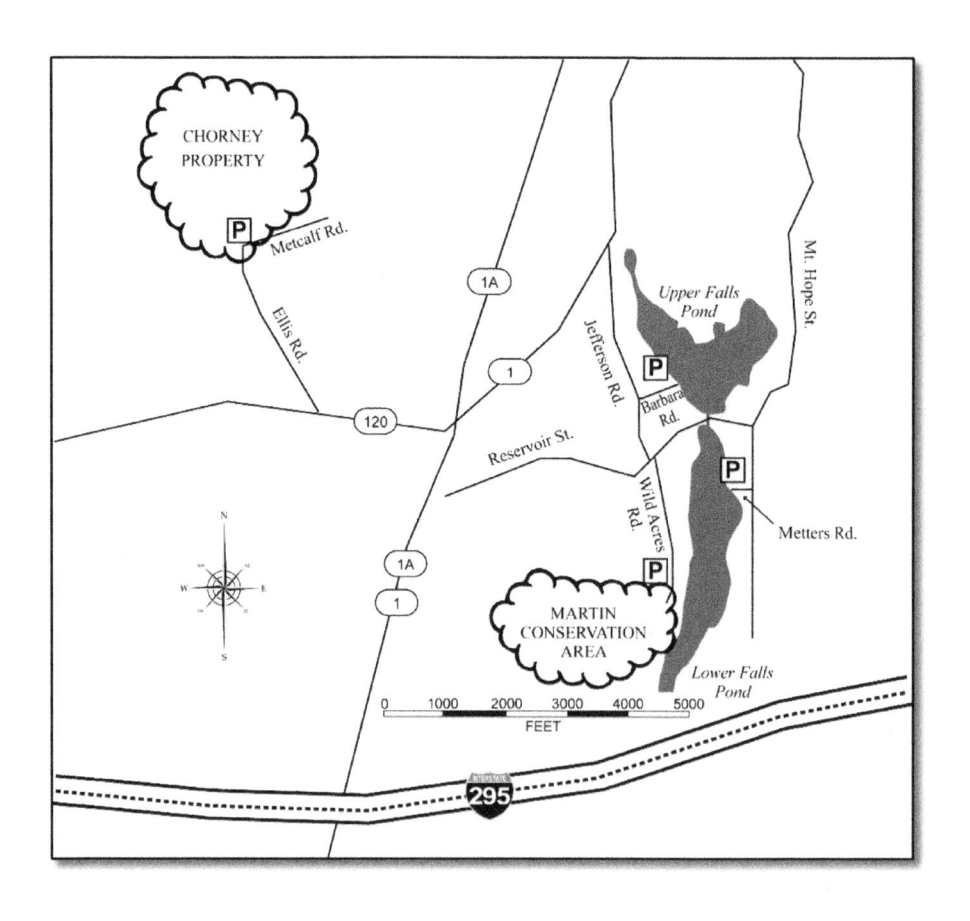

NORTH ATTLEBORO

Chorney Property

Features: 80 acres, hay fields with wooded trails. Seven Mile River flows through property.

Trail Map: N/A

GPS Coordinates: 41°58'26.04"N 71°21'04.80"W

Directions: Ellis Rd. and Metcalf Rd. From intersection of Rts.1, 1A and 120, go west onto Hoppin Hill Rd. (Rt.120) for 0.5 miles to Ellis Rd on the right, travel 0.5 miles to intersection of Ellis and Metcalf Rd. and look for trail kiosk on the left.

Cost: Free.

Bathrooms: Not available.

Best Time to Visit: Year round, may be wet in spring.

Trail Conditions: Unimproved marked dirt trails.

Distance: Under two miles of trail.

Parking: Space for at least six cars.

The Chorney Property is essentially a "three-hayfields" sanctuary connected by a few wooded trails. Part of the Seven Mile river flows through the property and the open land status helps protect the aquifer which feeds into the Attleboro Manchester reservoir. This is the part of the city with farms and horse barns, and is not part of the nearby dense retail development. I have road biked through here and you would swear that you were in Vermont. It has a lovely rural character. There are many well-to-do homes in the area, yet the farms and fields convey the feeling of being in another place and time.

Many thanks to Eagle Scout Christian Desrochers, who created this trail. Twenty-one landmark posts are situated in various places throughout the trail. The kiosk map describes what each landmark post represents.

I had walked almost the complete perimeter when one of the land posts pointed toward the woods. This led to a trampled down path for about 400 feet. Blazes on the trees indicated the way. The path was not always clear and at times I almost turned back. I encountered a few

NORTH ATTLEBORO

ladders next to trees which indicated deer hunting stands, but no hunters were in sight. Hunting is permitted on conservation land in North Attleboro. Observe the guidelines of always wearing blaze orange during hunting seasons. (Bill Luther)

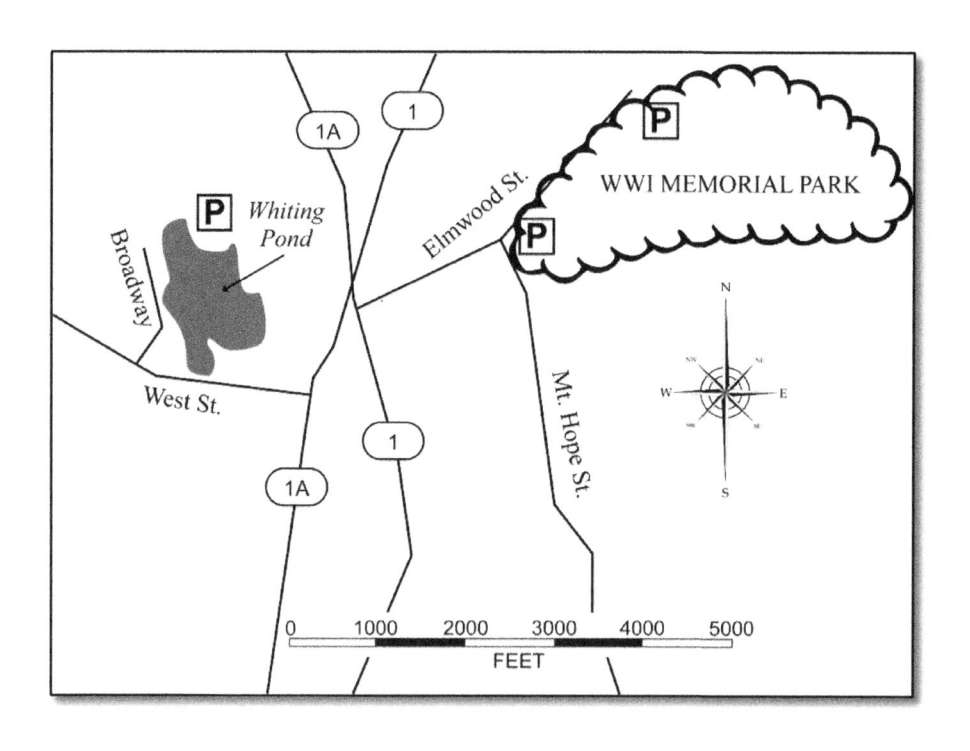

NORTH ATTLEBORO

NORTH ATTLEBORO

Whiting Pond

Features: Small pond for kayaks, canoes and fishing.

Trail Map: N/A

GPS Coordinates: 41°59'41.08"N 71°20'14.44"W

Directions: Broadway St. From intersection of Rts.106 and 1A in Plainville, travel 1 mile south on Rt.1A to right onto West St. 0.4 miles down, turn right onto Broadway. 0.2 mile on your right is parking and access to Whiting Pond.

Cost: Free.

Bathrooms: Not available.

NORTH ATTLEBORO

Best Time to Visit: April-October.

Trail Conditions: Public boat ramp to pond, no trails, no motorized boats allowed.

Distance: 31 acre pond.

Parking: For about 12 cars.

Whiting Pond is a small body of water in the headwaters of the Ten Mile River located just a little north of the downtown center of North Attleboro. A large neighborhood surrounds the pond.

The Conservation area is very small, perhaps less than an acre. This is a postage-stamp sized park. The borders are fenced off. This would be a nice spot for a picnic or just to sit here in a lawn chair and to admire the view of the pond on a warm sunny day. Besides a little trash, the area is well kept up. (Bill Luther)

Plainville

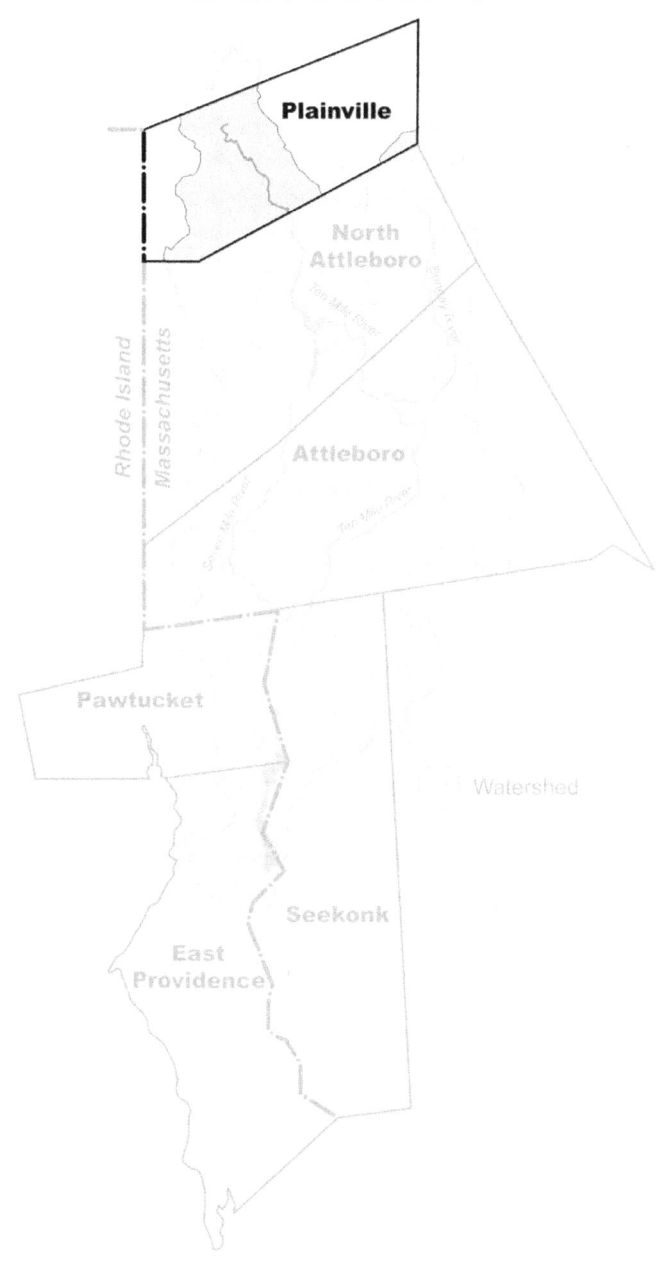

PLAINVILLE

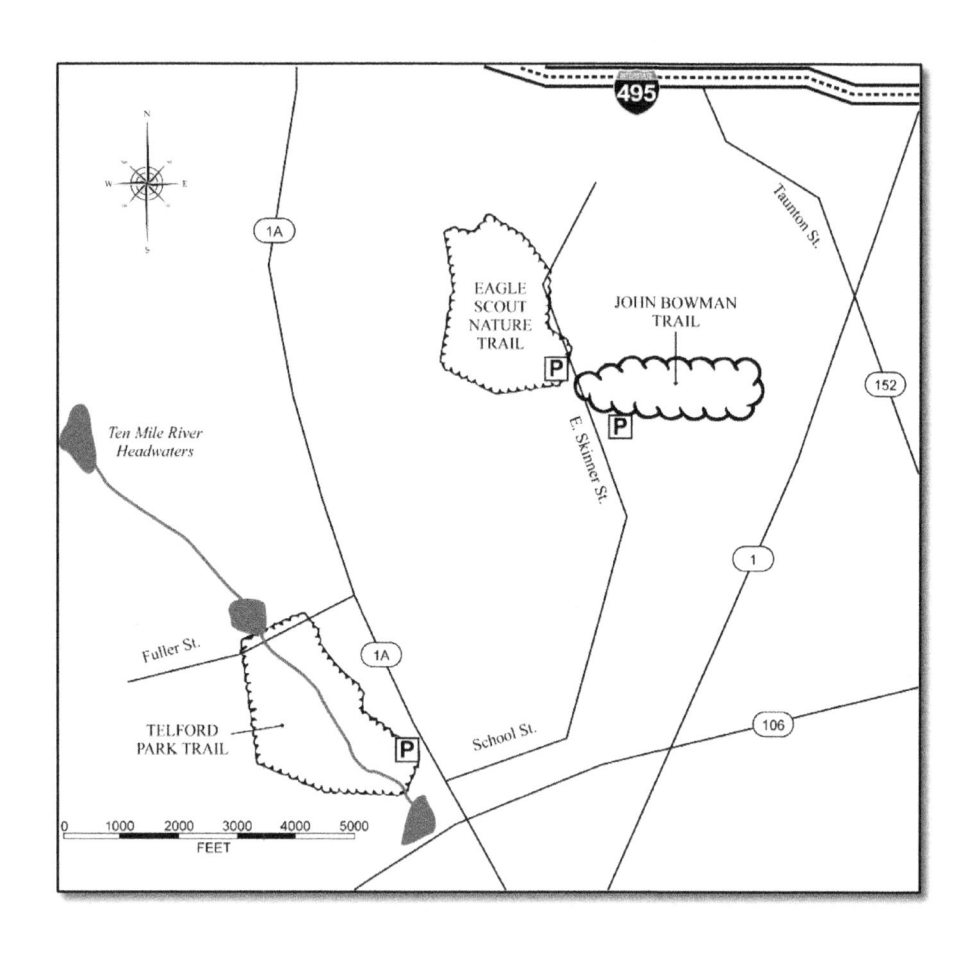

PLAINVILLE

Telford Park Trail

Features: Views of Ten Mile River, path along old railtrail.

Trail Map: Search "Plainville Open Space and Recreation"

GPS Coordinates: 42°00'20.14"N 71°20'15.45"W

Directions: 142 South St. (Rt.1A). From intersection of Rt.106 and Rt.1A, drive north 0.1 mile to old town hall and ball fields, Plainville Pond, Telford Park.

Cost: Free.

PLAINVILLE

Bathrooms: When events are ongoing.

Best Time to Visit: Summer, winter, fall. Trails extremely wet at times, especially in spring.

Trail Conditions: Marked trail, (some markers have been removed) some wet areas, some sections of old rail line, hard-packed dirt for much of the trail. Not ADA accessible. Short amount of road walking on Fuller St. to complete loop.

Distance: Two mile marked, loop trail.

Parking: Behind old town hall building; parking may be difficult when sporting events are scheduled.

The Ten Mile River flows behind the old and new Plainville town halls as well as the Public Library. A newly-marked trail travels from behind Telford Park north to Fuller Street. On-road walking on Fuller St. is necessary to cross over the stream and back onto the trail that will take you in a loop to the back of Telford Park.

Access the trail by crossing the small footbridge (step up and back down) at the back of the soccer field at Telford Park. A single trail leads out to an intersection, where you can travel a loop trail either to the right or left. Both directions will bring you back to the same point. Along the way are multiple small ponds, and a stream crossing, providing views of the Ten Mile River close to its headwaters. (MTH)

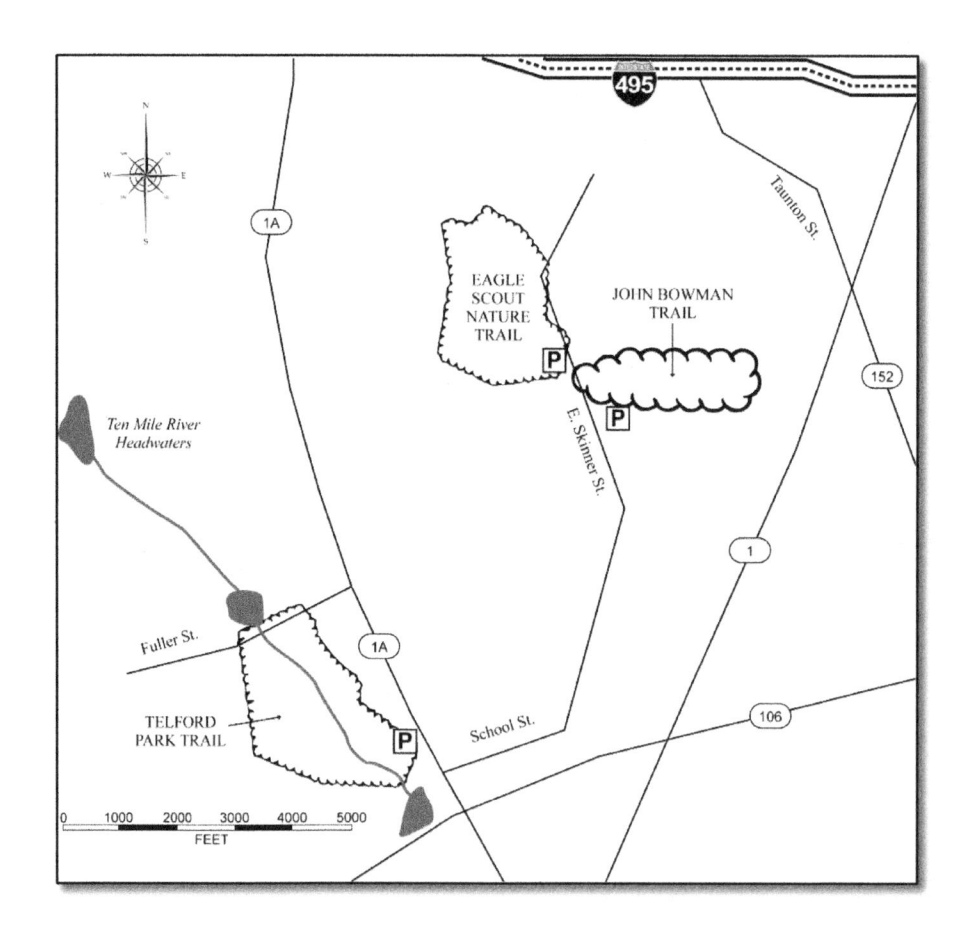

PLAINVILLE

PLAINVILLE

Eagle Scout Nature Trail

Features: Marked trail, small streams, eskers, access to the Warner Trail.

Trail Map: Search "Plainville Open Space and recreation"

GPS Coordinates: 42°01'30.43"N 71°19'43.07"W

Directions: 153 Everett Skinner St. Across from Beagle Club. From Rts.106 and 1A in Plainville, travel 0.1 miles north to School St. on the

PLAINVILLE

right, go 1.1 miles to end of School St. at intersection with George/E. Skinner St., then turn left. 0.5 miles down, just before the Beagle Club, which is on the right, is the Eagle Scout property on the left.

Cost: Free.

Bathrooms: None available.

Best Time to Visit: Year round.

Trail Conditions: Marked trail, packed dirt.

Distance: Loop trail, about two miles, with additional trails.

Parking: Space for at least eight cars in packed dirt parking lot.

A large network of trails is available in this area, but we followed the smaller loop trail that took us next to the small stream that flows through the property. The area has several eskers, which are long, winding ridges of coarse gravel, typically formed by glaciers. The eskers provided some challenging climbs, but the water bars helped with the footing. The trail has been marked, but some intersections are somewhat confusing. We never were terribly lost, just slightly confused a few times.

The streams were quite lovely, but tend to dry up in the summer. Lots of stone walls add interest and made this a really nice, mostly easy walk. (MTH)

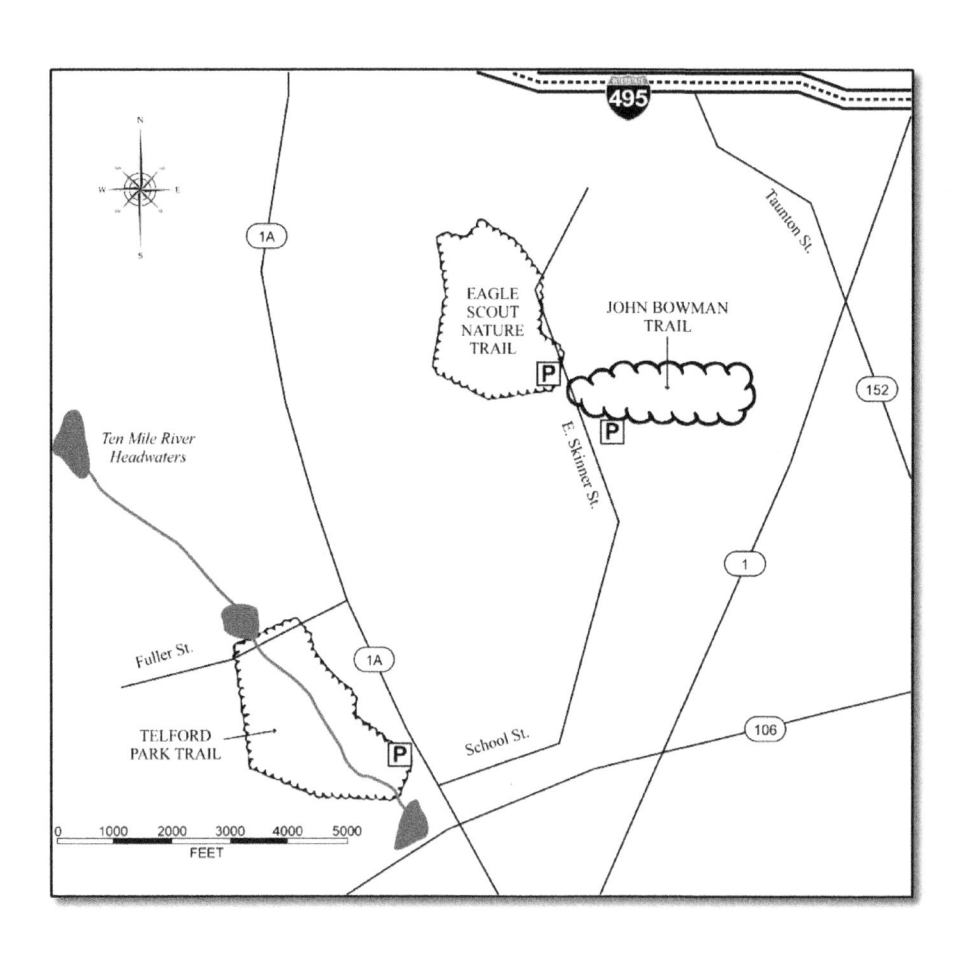

PLAINVILLE

PLAINVILLE

John Bowman Trail

Features: Out and back trail with pond views, brook crossing.

Trail Map: Search "Plainville Open Space and recreation"

GPS Coordinates: 42°01'17.31"N 71°19'39.32"W

PLAINVILLE

Directions: Directly next to Little League ball field on Everett Skinner St. From Rts.106 and 1A in Plainville, travel 0.1 miles north to School St. on the right, go 1.1 miles to end of School St. at intersection with George/E. Skinner St., then turn left, look for Little League field, 0.3 miles on the right.

Cost: Free.

Bathrooms: None Available.

Best Time to Visit: Year round.

Trail Conditions: Clear dirt track, some rocks and roots, steep uphill near view of pond.

Distance: Two miles round trip, out and back.

Parking: At Little League Ball field parking—limited access when games are underway.

Many towns have trails that abut their recreation fields, and Plainville is no exception. The Little League ball field on E. Skinner Rd., quite near the Eagle Scout trail (just a little farther down on the opposite side of the street), has a clear track accessible just beyond the parking lot at the Little League ball field.

This is mostly a woods walk, with a small, pretty brook that crosses underneath the trail by way of a culvert, near the beginning of the trail. Enjoy views (in winter when the leaves are down) of a lake that abuts Rt.1, which is where we turned around. The trail offers some

PLAINVILLE

varied terrain, somewhat rocky, with only a few roots, and one or two small trees that have fallen across the path. The trees are no real barrier for walkers, just something that will discourage motorized off-road vehicles.

In the late fall we found a few beech trees stubbornly holding on to their foliage. We also came across a large construction site directly next to the trail near where we turned around. We walked in total nearly two miles, round trip.

Additional trails are available, as referenced on the town trail map. (MTH)

Seekonk

SEEKONK

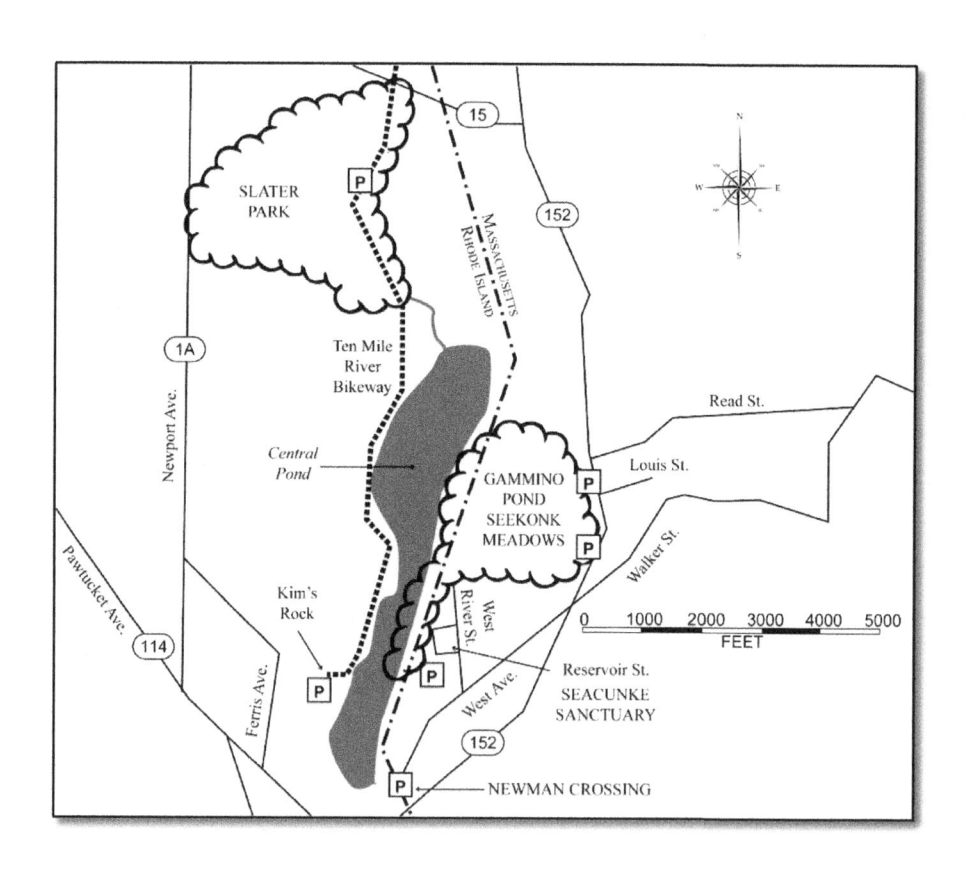

SEEKONK

Seekonk Meadows

Features: 60-acre conservation land behind library, multiple trails, option for water views at Gammino Pond, meadows, woodland, picnic tables (handicapped accessible), Veteran's Memorial.

Trail Map: N/A

GPS Coordinates: 41°51'11.86"N 71°19'45.70"W

Directions: 410 Newman Ave. (Seekonk Public Library) Rt.152 in Seekonk.

SEEKONK

Cost: Free.

Bathrooms: When library is open.

Best Time to Visit: Year round.

Trail Conditions: Grassy meadow trails mowed in summer months, graveled paths.

Distance: 0.75 miles around the Meadows area.

Parking: At Seekonk Library, large parking area.

The trail head begins at the back of the Seekonk Public Library. Beware of "people trails" in this area, keep to the marked trails. The Meadows has open fields and mowed paths.

The Library and Meadows area exist on land which was once a landfill, closed in 1978. The area was capped and is monitored for gas emissions. A gazebo offers a spot where the town holds some civic events during the year.

Adjacent to the Meadows is Gammino Pond, which was once a sand and gravel operation which closed many years ago. The pond is five acres large and was created during excavation. In years past local kids rode bikes here and swam in the cool waters during the summer months. A rougher path (not always easy) circles Gammino Pond.

Three parcels of open space land, all connected, are behind the Seekonk Library, and together make for some great hiking. Gammino Pond has 62 acres, and the Meadows has nine acres and Seacunke

SEEKONK

Sanctuary (connected by a path to the Meadows and Gammino Pond) has 17 acres. The Meadows is administered by the Library Trust and the Pond and Seacunke Sanctuary are overseen by the Seekonk Conservation Commission. These pieces of land are all within the Ten Mile River watershed and are all connected. (Bill Luther, Ernie Germani, MTH)

SEEKONK

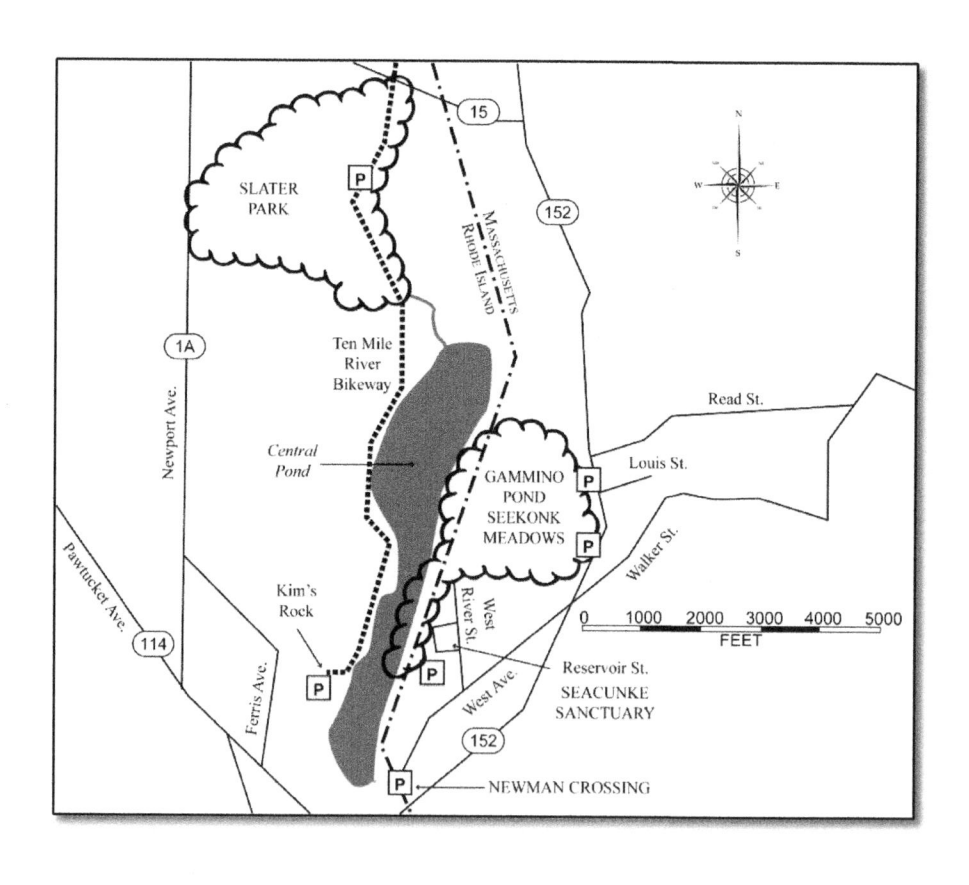

SEEKONK

Gammino Pond Conservation Area

Features: Water views, loop trail around pond, connecting trails to Seekonk Meadows, Seacunke Sanctuary.

Trail Map: Search "Seekonk Rec Gammino Pond trail map"

GPS Coordinates: 41°51'15.69"N 71°19'43.41"W

SEEKONK

Directions: 410 Newman Ave (Rt.152) Seekonk Library, or 75 yards north of library on Newman Ave (Rt.152) directly across from Louis St.

Cost: Free.

Bathrooms: When library is open.

Best Time to Visit: Year round.

Trail Conditions: Gammino Pond has a narrow dirt track around the pond which can be rough in places. An Easy Walk from parking area north of the library to the shore of the pond. More challenging conditions on trail around the pond.

Distance: 1.5 mile loop.

Parking: At Seekonk Library, or 75 yards north of library on Newman Ave. (parking for up to 10 vehicles.)

Gammino Pond was once a sand and gravel operation and closed many years ago. The pond is five acres large and was created during excavation. In the past local kids rode bikes here, and swam in the cool waters during the summer months.

There are three parcels of land behind the Seekonk Library which have some great hiking. Gammino Pond has 62 acres, Seacunke Sanctuary has 17 acres and the Meadows has 9 acres. The Meadows is administered by the Library Trust and the former two by the Seekonk Conservation Commission. Along with this the City of East

SEEKONK

Providence's Water Board owns most of the adjacent land along the shoreline of Central Pond. These pieces of land are all within the Ten Mile River watershed and are all connected. Seacunke Sanctuary is part of land donated to the Town, including most of the Marian Farm. Efforts to secure and consolidate this conservation area have been ongoing for decades. The trails have officially been open during the last decade.

If you parked at the trail head just north of the library, go straight ahead and find the start of the blue-blazed trail. If you start in the library parking lot, face the Meadows and turn to your immediate right and walk 100 yards down a small dip in the land, then go right and then left to pick up the blue-blazed trail. You will pass Gammino Pond to your left. Enjoy the views across the large pond. Farther along is a cove to your right which is the mouth of Coles Brook, draining Caratunk Refuge and Ledgemont Country Club. The water is murky and unappealing.

The path crisscrosses the Mass/RI state border. The City of East Providence owns a certain border along the water which was once part of a public water supply system for the city, closed in 1967. The land is public and open for passive recreation. The border between the two states is unmarked. The woods are open without thick undergrowth or blowdowns, a mid-aged hardwood forest.

After walking above the river's steep banks, drop down a short embankment where you will find a spot on the pond which may have a make-shift boat landing.

SEEKONK

I consider this area and view of the river to be the highlight of the trip. I once walked here on a frigid winter day and heard the ice on the pond loudly groan as it expanded. It is a short distance across to the nearby shoreline, where you can toss a rock and nearly hit the far shore.

The blue-blazed, mile-long trail is an introduction to the Conservation area. Unless you can follow a trail map and have a good sense of direction, you should just get a taste for the area. There are several miles of other marked trails with red and white blazes. The borders are Newman Ave. to your east and the impassable Ten Mile River to your west. (Bill Luther, Ernie Germani, MTH)

SEEKONK

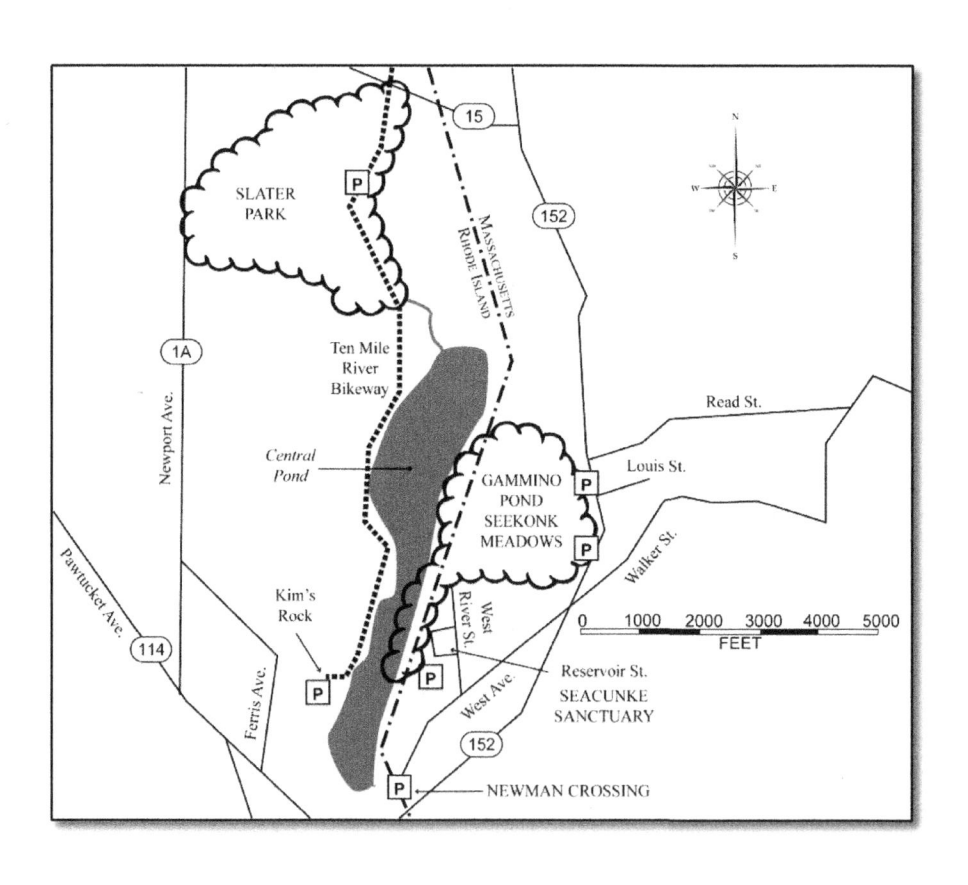

94

Seacunke Sanctuary

Features: Water views, connecting trails to Gammino Pond, Seekonk Meadows.

Trail Map: N/A

GPS Coordinates: 41°50'57.02"N 71°20'21.11"W

Directions: From Seekonk Library, 410 Newman Ave., drive 0.25 miles on Rt.152 to West Ave. on the right, travel 0.3 miles to W. River St. on the right. 0.1 miles down, take your first left onto

SEEKONK

Reservoir St., or the next, Dexter St. (the road is actually a loop). The sanctuary is at the far end of either road, the dirt connector between the two roads.

From East Providence area: Rt.152 just north of Central pond just north of the state line into Seekonk from East Providence, take an immediate left onto West Ave., then turn left onto W. River St., travel to Reservoir or Dexter, turn left, follow to the dirt road.

Cost: Free.

Bathrooms: None available.

Best Time to Visit: Year round.

Trail Conditions: Packed dirt, loop trail.

Distance: 0.5 miles within Sanctuary itself, additional miles of trail around Gammino Pond, Seekonk Meadows.

Parking: For two or three cars. On Reservoir or Dexter St. where it becomes dirt road, in front of tall, wooden Seacuncke Sanctuary sign.

Seacuncke Sanctuary is a quiet, wooded parcel on the east side of Central Pond, with occasional clearings of tall grass. In these small clearings you will notice some rather large ant mounds. The sanctuary itself is in Seekonk and the remainder of the land is actually in East Providence.

From the small parking area by the trail head sign follow the narrow trail into the sanctuary. Stay to the left at the split and you will soon notice some ant mounds. The trail to the right leads to the Seekonk Trail and you can return on this trail. After staying to the left, look for a wood post on the left of the trail. That is the approximate state line. The entrance trail then comes to an end.

The trail to the left dead ends at a point on Central Pond that is suitable for kayak or canoe launching. The trail to the right is the Seekonk Trail and follows the shore of Central Pond for about 0.5 miles (1 mile out and back). The trail ends at the gully and blue trail intersection of Gammino Pond. There are some narrower, less defined trails along this stretch. The property is rather quiet, very peaceful, and good for bird watching. (Ernie Germani, MTH)

SEEKONK

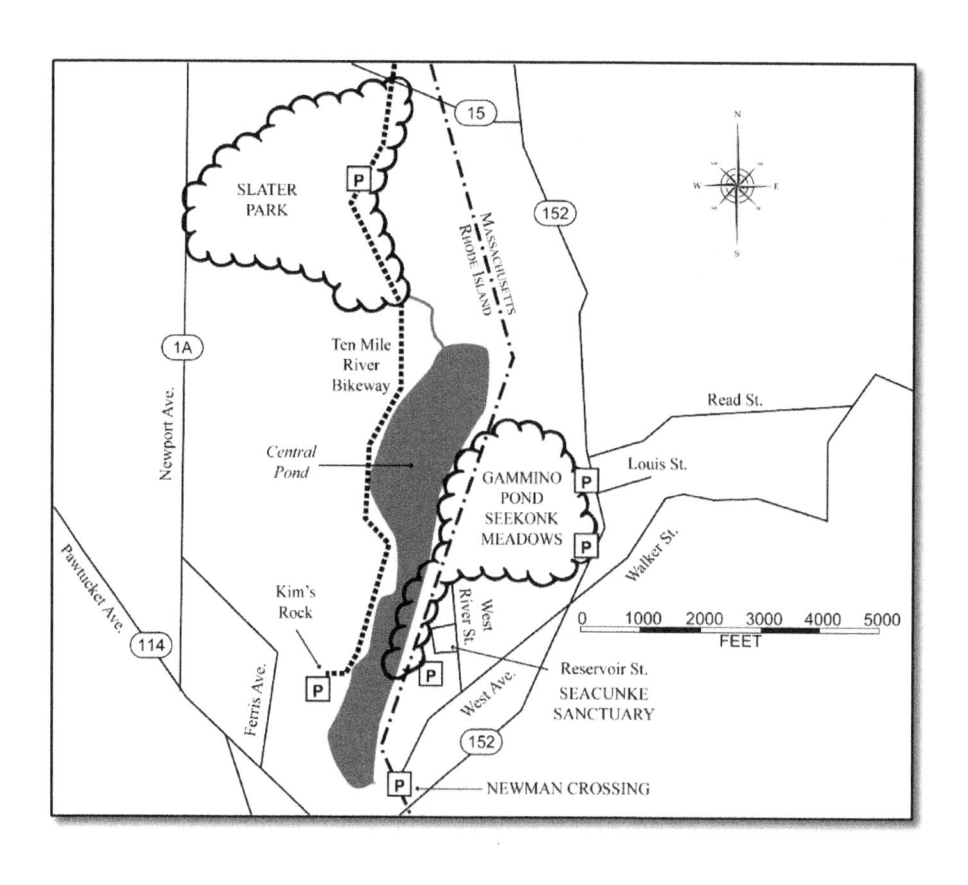

SEEKONK

Newman Crossing

Features: Canoe launch, access to Central Pond.

Trail Maps: N/A

GPS Coordinates: 41°50'33.13"N 71°20'27.29"W

Directions: Travel south on Rt.152 for 1 mile past Seekonk Library (410 Newman Ave.) to just before the bridge at boundary between Seekonk and East Providence, (across from Arcade Ave. on the left). Look for West Ave. on the right. Park on West Ave., on the left,

SEEKONK

nearest the pond, boat launch is directly adjacent to bridge on Rt.152 on the Seekonk, or north, side of the bridge.

Cost: None.

Bathrooms: None available.

Best Time to Visit: Spring to fall.

Trail Conditions: Suitable for kayaks and canoes. No strong current.

Distance: No hiking, boat access only to Central Pond.

Parking: On West Rd., adjacent to the bridge on 152 between Seekonk and East Providence. Parking for two or three cars, next to Rt.152.

As you paddle northward away from the road, you will see an old dam foundation and wheel house which once powered the mills on Central Pond. These structures are from a bygone era. As you round the corner you'll pass the last houses in sight in the upper stretches. The river narrows and deepens as you paddle for another 0.5 mile.

Soon you will approach a large wide open area where swans rule. They will note your presence and drift off. Swans can be aggressive when raising young. A few coves reach into the woods. Conservation land, including Seacunke Sanctuary, is off to the right. In the shallows in the far northeastern corner is a stone marker which at one time was a state boundary marker. This is a vast open area where few houses are visible.

SEEKONK

Unfortunately, an invasive plant mats the surface of the water thru the summer making it almost impassable. In higher water you could paddle an uncertain route which would bring you into the walled sections of Slater Park, on the opposite, western side of the pond from the Seekonk shoreline. You may need to poke around false routes until you actually find your way upriver. Tree stumps are just below the surface of Central Pond. Proceed with caution.

Most people turn around once they hit the weeds and return downriver. We, however, reached Slater Park when we paddled in the fall. You can paddle almost all the way to Pawtucket Country Club. Past this point trees will probably stop your upstream progress. This area known as Central Pond can be very quiet and peaceful.

On the opposite bank to the west is the Ten Mile River Greenway where you may see a few people strolling on the paved trail. You are not far from the Ten Mile River Greenway walking path as you paddle south and return to your car. (Bill Luther)

SEEKONK

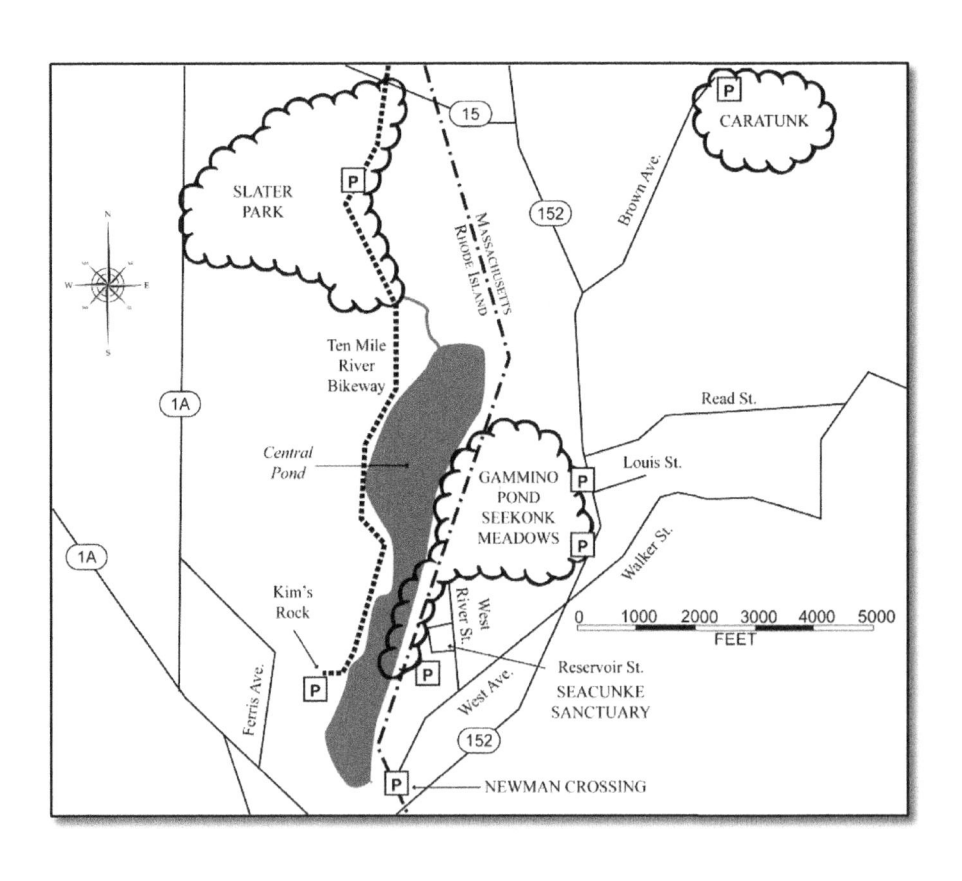

SEEKONK

Caratunk Wildlife Refuge

Features: Views of Coles Brook, several bridge crossings, Muskrat pond, Ice Pond, stone walls, loop trails, limited views.

Trail Map: Search "RI Audubon Caratunk"

GPS Coordinates: 41°52'30.21"N 71°19'16.30"W

Directions: 301 Brown Ave. From the Seekonk Library on Rt.152, travel north on Rt.152 for 0.8 miles. Seekonk Middle School will be on the left. Just past it, turn right onto Brown Ave. Caratunk is 0.8 miles down on the right.

Cost: Not required.

SEEKONK

Bathrooms: None available, unless program is running.

Best Time to Visit: Year round, dawn to dusk.

Trail Conditions: Marked trails, boardwalks.

Distance: 200 acres, 1.8 mile perimeter trail.

Parking: Ample parking for 20 cars.

On a visit to Caratunk we first encountered the wooden bridge that spanned Coles Brook, a tributary of the Ten Mile River. We stood on the bridge and watched the high water of early spring rush under us. I wanted to see fish running upstream but this is not a spawning river.

We emerged into the open fields and walked alongside a stonewall. Heading back into the woods we found Muskrat Pond which was full at high water. I'm told that otters and muskrats can be seen in this pond. Walking just a short way farther we found another smaller pond called Ice Pond, with stone-cut retaining walls.

A gentle slope travels toward the power lines. We got into the open view area and decided to walk on another outer loop trail. There were some low spots with a boardwalk which just barely floats above the puddles. Here we decided to turn around.

We came out at the power lines. This is the high ground on the trip and you can see Ledgemont Country Club and some nearby, newly-built houses. This area is filled with thick briars which force travelers to stay on the trail.

SEEKONK

We walked into the fields and noticed some white objects sitting on high metal poles. These were multiple bird feeding stations which looked like modern high tech listening devices. The small Audubon staff keeps track of popular bird food for certain times of year. We saw a few wrens flying and perching on the poles. (Bill Luther)

SEEKONK

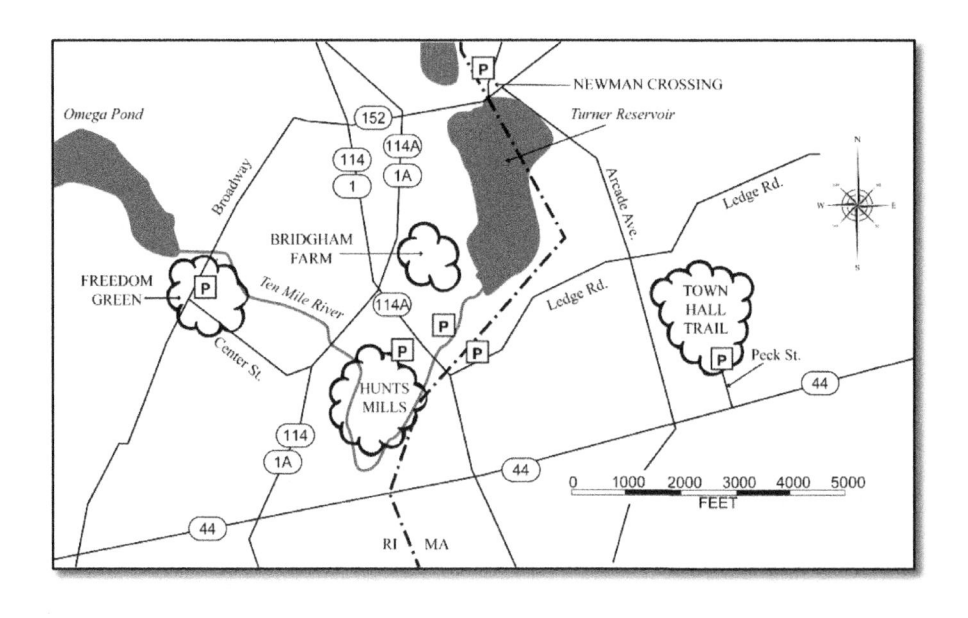

SEEKONK

Town Hall Runnins River Trail

Features: ADA accessible trail, boardwalks through wetlands.

Trail Map: Search "Seekonk Land Trust Runnins river trail map"

GPS Coordinates: 41°49'49.68"N 71°19'28.79"W

Directions: 100 Peck St., behind Seekonk Town Hall. From intersection of Rts.95 and 195, travel on Rt.195 East for 2.5 miles to the Rt.114/Pawtucket Ave. exit, travel north for 0.6 miles to Rt.44, turn right onto Rt.44. Travel 1.6 miles to Peck St. on the left. Turn left, drive a short ways to a traffic circle and bear to your right, at the Seekonk Town Hall.

SEEKONK

Cost: Free.

Bathrooms: When Town Hall is open.

Best Time to Visit: Year-round, trail is not plowed.

Trail Conditions: ADA accessible, packed stone dust, and boardwalk.

Distance: 0.5 miles with additional longer walking options.

Parking: At Seekonk Town Hall for about 25 cars. Park at back of lot.

The Runnins River, or Town Hall Trail is located behind some of the municipal buildings and Newman YMCA just off Rt.44, Taunton Ave. Park as far back from the town hall as you can and walk toward the woods. The Animal shelter is to your right, where you will hear dogs barking. You will soon see several picnic benches and a kiosk with info about the walk. This is the beginning of the red trail. Your walk should take about 25–30 minutes at casual speeds.

After traveling on several trails for this book, I would have to say that this is the best maintained and blazed path that I have probably ever seen. It is ADA compliant and anyone with a mobility issue or who is wheelchair bound would have little problem accessing this trail in clear weather. In some sections the trees are metal-plate blazed every 12 feet of travel. Some sections are packed, crushed stone dust. The boardwalk and bridges are a marvelous addition to an area that was once inaccessible wetlands.

I grew up here and have many memories of this area. My father once called this the Bull Field, which has its own story. I recall running in the woods playing Capture the Flag and sledding here during the winter in my youth. This was the Woods.

I noticed a vernal pool with a viewing platform. Vernal pools are full of life in early spring.

The red trail is primarily boardwalk and bog bridges. Prickly briar bushes stop most hikers. but because the trail is now elevated by a bog bridge, it is possible to walk right past the briars. Another section of trail has wooden plank bridges. These are not ADA accessible. They are connected by cables and anchored to stakes in the ground. This was a low lying wetlands and probably often floods early in the year.

I got off the bridges to walk by the river, only ten feet away from the trail. Soon I approached a bridge spanning the river for about a thirty feet distance and stood a good three feet off the water's surface. This is an impressive bridge which was meant to last. I have been told that although the bridge appears to be composed of wood and metal it is actually fiberglass constructed, snap-on pieces which are durable and lightweight. Regardless, it is the only way over the river. The river had a good flow the day I visited. It was about 10 feet across and maybe 12 inches deep.

In the late summer months I would not want to be near here at twilight. The mosquitoes would probably eat a person alive.

The trail leads to Arcade Ave., where most people will turn around, content to have a short walk. Within a 0.25 mile walk is Seekonk High School and the Turner Reservoir Trail. Connecting to

SEEKONK

this area will extend the walk to 4–5 miles.

This was another quiet walk where you would see few visitors. The Town Hall and Turner Reservoir trails would be great places to get warmed up with snow shoes or cross country skis. Such are the benefits of knowing where local trails are found. (Bill Luther, MTH)

SEEKONK

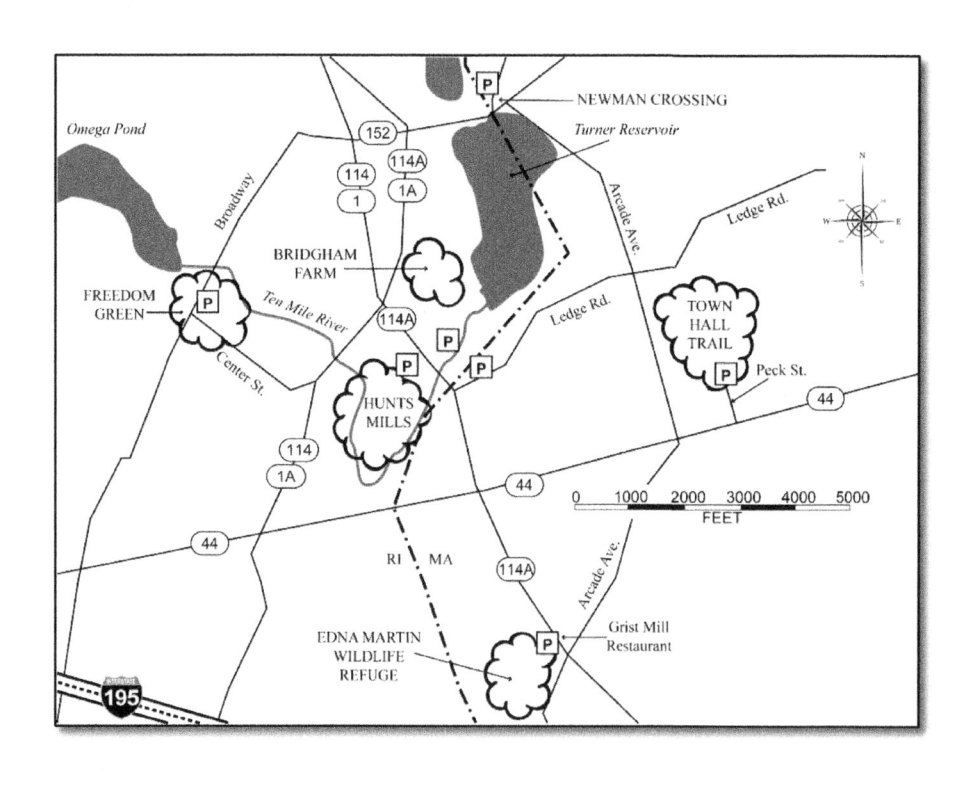

SEEKONK

Edna Martin Wildlife Refuge

Features: Boardwalks, Burr Pond.

Trail Map: N/A

GPS Coordinates: 41°49'01.64"N 71°20'14.29"W

Directions: Across the street from 351 Fall River Ave. From intersection of Rts.95 and 195 in Providence, travel east on Rt.195 for 1.2 miles to the Rt.44 exit, heading northeast. Go 2 miles on Rt.44 to a right onto Fall River Ave./Rt.114A. Travel 0.5 miles to the American Legion Post on your right and the Grist Mill Restaurant on your left. Within 50 feet you can turn right into the easy-to-miss entrance across from the Firefly golf course entrance.

SEEKONK

Cost: Free.

Bathrooms: None Available. Check at American Legion Hall or Grist Mill Restaurant.

Best Time to Visit: Year Round.

Trail Conditions: Wide, unblazed, packed dirt trails.

Distance: 0.7 mile loop trail.

Parking: For 8-10 cars. Use extreme caution exiting the lot!!

The Martin Wildlife Refuge is a small, 35-acre Seekonk Land Trust site which opened about 12 years ago because of a land donation from Edna Martin. She was a 9th-generation Seekonk resident who spent most of her life as an Art director at the Lincoln School. She was known for her love of animals. The area is designated for passive recreation and quiet walking. Dog walking, horseback riding, motor vehicles, picnics, hunting, fishing and trapping are discouraged.

Two kiosks are at the entrance. Some graffiti can be found along the trails, but the trails themselves are very clean of trash. Use extra caution when exiting the lot since sight lines are poor when entering into oncoming traffic.

The trail is unblazed, however you cannot miss the 15 foot wide paths, which may have served as roads many years ago. The ground on these paths is packed dirt, and in late fall a thick layer of leaves covers the trail.

SEEKONK

When you first enter the woods you will see a rock with a plaque noting this is the Nancy Messinger Trail. Nancy was the Land Trust President in 2003 when Edna Martin made this land donation. This is an old-growth forest which seems unnatural for an area that has so much retail development nearby. This is the heart of the historic center of South Seekonk, where grist mills once served the population. Many nearby homes date back over 100 years.

Burr Pond, within this property, has a catch-and-release fishing only policy, due to high mercury and bacteria levels. I can never recall anyone swimming here, but it may have been used for ice skating at one time. A dam holds back the water of the pond. At one time there was a covered bridge on a road over the river which collapsed during the Blizzard of 1978.

The pond is a nice place to quietly think about things while you are away from the hustle and bustle of life. A few benches are available, overlooking the water. The walk is short but it can be a quick get-away from your normal routine. (Bill Luther)

East Providence

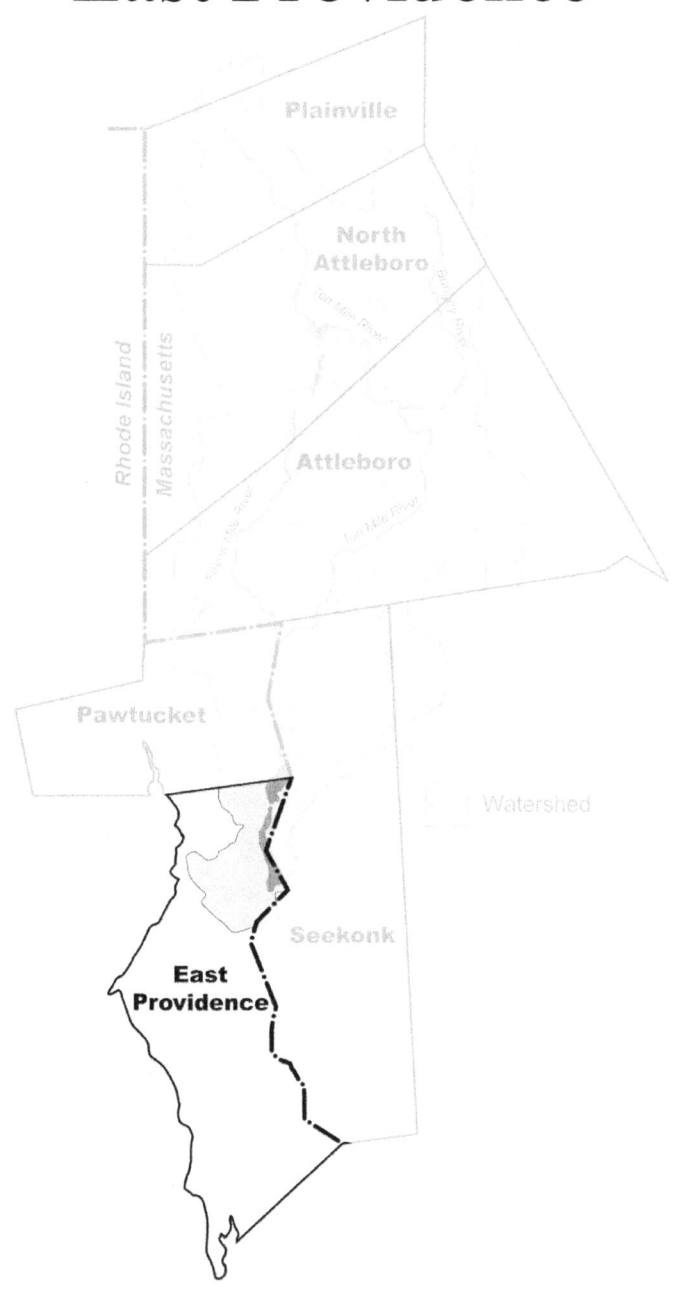

EAST PROVIDENCE

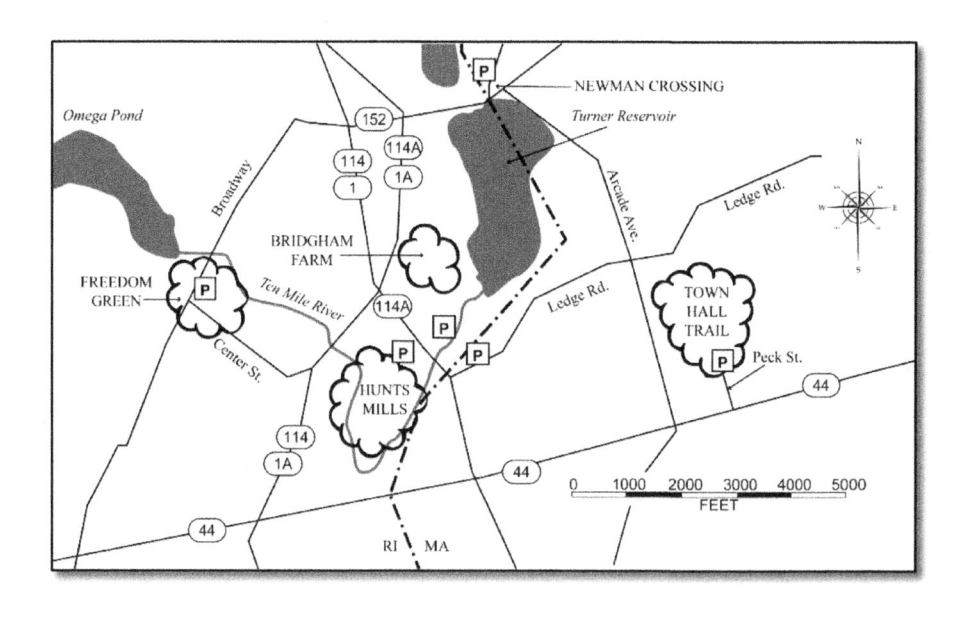

EAST PROVIDENCE

Hunt's Mills

Features: Fish ladder, waterfalls, loop trail, historical buildings, views of Ten Mile River, easy walk to Turner Reservoir trails (across the street).

Trail Map: N/A

GPS Coordinates: 41°49'40.07"N 71°20'45.12"W

EAST PROVIDENCE

Directions: 65 Hunts Mills Rd., Rumford (East Providence). From intersection of Rts.95 and 195 in Providence, travel east on Rt.195 for 1.2 miles to the Rt.44 exit, heading northeast. Go 2 miles on Rt.44 to left onto Fall River Ave./Rt.114A. Follow Rt.114A north into East Providence 0.5 miles, turn left onto Hunts Mills Rd.

From Rt.152 in Seekonk, cross the state line into Rhode Island, (East Providence) and travel 0.5 miles to the next light (Rt.1A) turn left. Travel 0.5 miles to intersection with Rt.114A, at the light turn left onto Rt.114A, travel 0.2 miles, look for Hunts Mills Rd. on the right. Drive to end of road, at the waterfall.

Cost: Free.

Bathrooms: Available only when Hunt House is open (second Sundays of month, 1–3 p.m.).

Best Time to Visit: Year round.

Trail Conditions: Well-marked, red-blazed loop trail along Ten Mile River, hard-packed earth. Canoe launch into Ten Mile River.

Distance: 0.8 mile loop trail, additional side trails.

Parking: At Hunt House and dam area.

Over the past 250 years Hunt's Mills has served many purposes. It is probably one of the more historically significant sites in East Providence. In fact this property is home to the East Providence

EAST PROVIDENCE

Historical Society. The historical society is at the John Hunt House, one of the oldest houses in the city, built in the mid-1700's.

This site has also been home to several mills dating back to the mid-1600's, including a sawmill and a grist mill. In the late 1800's a local private company (Rumford Chemical Works) set up a water company here to supply their mills and factories with water. In the mid-1920's the City of East Providence took over the water company, along with the Turner Reservoir, to supply the growing town with water until the town starting receiving its water from the Scituate Reservoir.

At the turn of the 20th century an amusement park was created next to the river to help offset the cost of running the water company. Most recently the fire department used this property as a training ground.

The trail head starts near the small parking area by the gazebo just to the right of the Hunt House. The red-blazed trail leads down a small set of stone stairs then winds through an area known as the Terrace Garden. At different times of year different shrubs and flowers bloom here, including mountain laurel.

Look for Sunset Rock along the trail. It tends to be a little overgrown in the summer months, but offers a good view of the river the rest of the year. Otter Rock is also along this trail, since otters have been spotted in this area. When the water levels are low on the river you will find inscriptions carved into the rocks in the early 1900's.

Remnants of the fire training facility are visible, including the old fire tower that was used for training and an old tanker. This area is currently being leased by the Ten Mile River Watershed Council. The group has been actively making improvements to the grounds in this area.

In the large grassy area behind the Hunt House there is a circle of granite blocks. These blocks represent where the carousel of the amusement park once stood.

The pump house (built in 1893) for the water department, is next to the Hunt House. Hunts Mills dam and waterfall are probably the highlight of this area, offering a wilderness feel in the midst of the city. This hike makes a nice companion to the Turner Reservoir hike. (Ernie Germani, MTH)

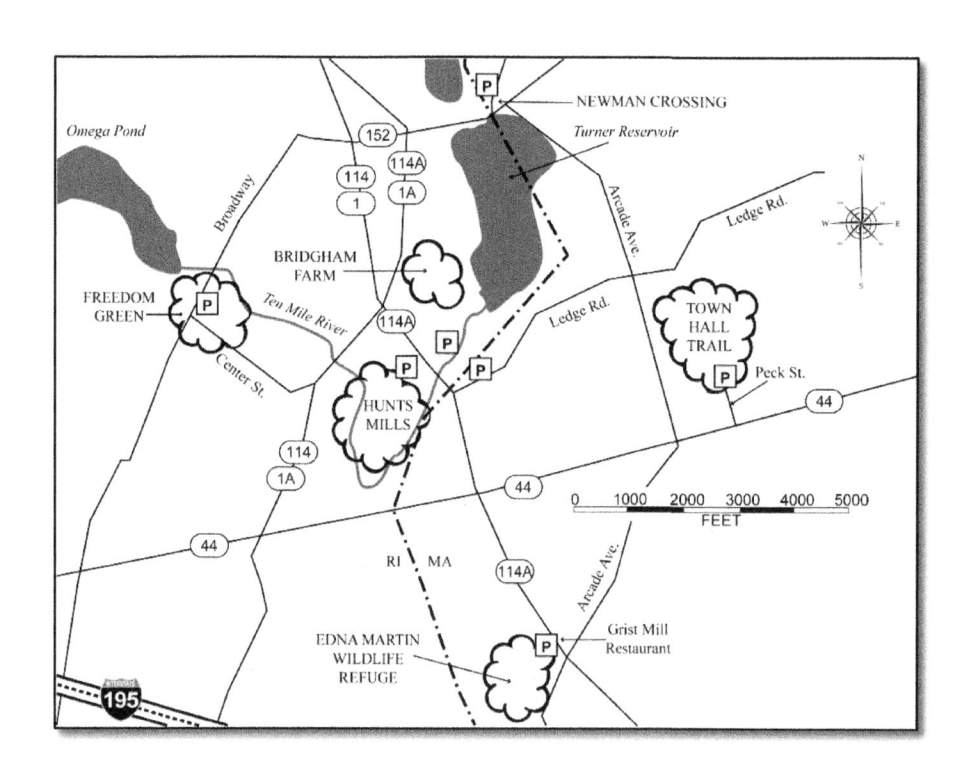

EAST PROVIDENCE

EAST PROVIDENCE

Turner Reservoir

Features: Loop trail, water views, bog bridge over river floodplain, some road walking to complete loop.

Trail Map: N/A

GPS Coordinates: 41°49'47.05" 71°20'36.94"W

Directions: 400 Pleasant St. From intersection of Rts.95 and 195 in Providence, travel east on Rt.195 for 1.2 miles to the Rt.44 exit, heading northeast. Go 2 miles on Rt.44 to left onto Fall River

EAST PROVIDENCE

Ave./Rt.114A. Follow Rt.114A north for 0.5 miles into East Providence. Parking is on the right.

From Rt.152 in Seekonk, cross the state line into Rhode Island, (East Providence) and travel 0.5 miles to the next light (Rt.1A) turn left. Travel 0.5 miles to intersection with Rt.114A, at the light turn left onto Rt.114A, travel 0.3 miles to parking on the left.

Cost: Free.

Bathrooms: None Available.

Best Time to Visit: Year Round.

Trail Conditions: Rooty, dirt track alongside the reservoir on East Providence side, sidewalk road crossing on Newman Ave (Rt.152) to Arcade Ave., more sidewalk travel to wooded path just north of Seekonk High School to complete loop, walking on woodland paths, boardwalks across swampy area, back to parking on Rt.114.

Distance: 2.7 miles, with additional trail available to view the Newman Oak at Bridgham Farm.

Parking: At 400 Pleasant St. for 5-6 cars, additional parking for 25 vehicles due east across the bridge under which flows the Ten Mile River) twenty yards away, on Rt.114A.

Most of the wooded trails around the reservoir are under the jurisdiction of the East Providence Water Commission. The commission owns the land from 10 feet to 150 feet above the shoreline. There is no fence separating the two state boundary lines here.

The trail has some rocks and places to jump over. Look out for poison ivy in spots near the trail. The path is blue blazed. On the Seekonk side of the loop, the forested wetlands are damp, and turtles and frogs probably begin their lives here in the spring. You would not be able to walk the trail if there wasn't a bridge. The trail is wide for its length until it reaches Arcade Ave. You will soon notice what seems to be a logging operation. Cut up logs are on both sides of the trail and many dead pine trees are still standing. This may have been the result of a storm microburst or blight. No trees block the trail.

Neighboring houses are quite nearby at some points. Be mindful of their right to privacy, and make an effort to reduce noise when in the area.

Either direction of travel around the reservoir requires walking along the bridge at the north end of the reservoir. Walking on the sidewalk along Arcade Ave. is also necessary when walking either direction of the loop trail.

The beauty of the Turner Reservoir is that no one has developed their homes to suggest that they have waterfront properties. You are not in the forest here. Just small clusters of trees line the shoreline. You will not reach heavy woods until you have walked almost 0.25 mile toward the Turner reservoir dam. The path can be narrow, marshy, and covered with roots that are a tripping hazard. Take care. Fishermen will fish along the berm which defines the dam placement. In the summer

EAST PROVIDENCE

fireflies light up the open meadows near the dam.

The Newman Oak is nearby in the Bridgham Farm property, where Samuel Newman is reputed to have given a sermon hundreds of years ago. Catch a view of the 15-foot-high dam, rushing water and nearby fish ladder before leaving to visit Bridgham Farm.

Near Rt.114 on the East Providence side is a forest canopy and it can feel like walking through a tunnel of trees. This hike is not a wilderness hike. The reservoir has toxic algae growth sometimes in the summer. For the rest of the year it is a jewel which calls for your attention. Ignore the road and traffic noise and you will find a peaceful place to get away from it all. (Bill Luther, Ernie Germani, Sue Stephenson, MTH)

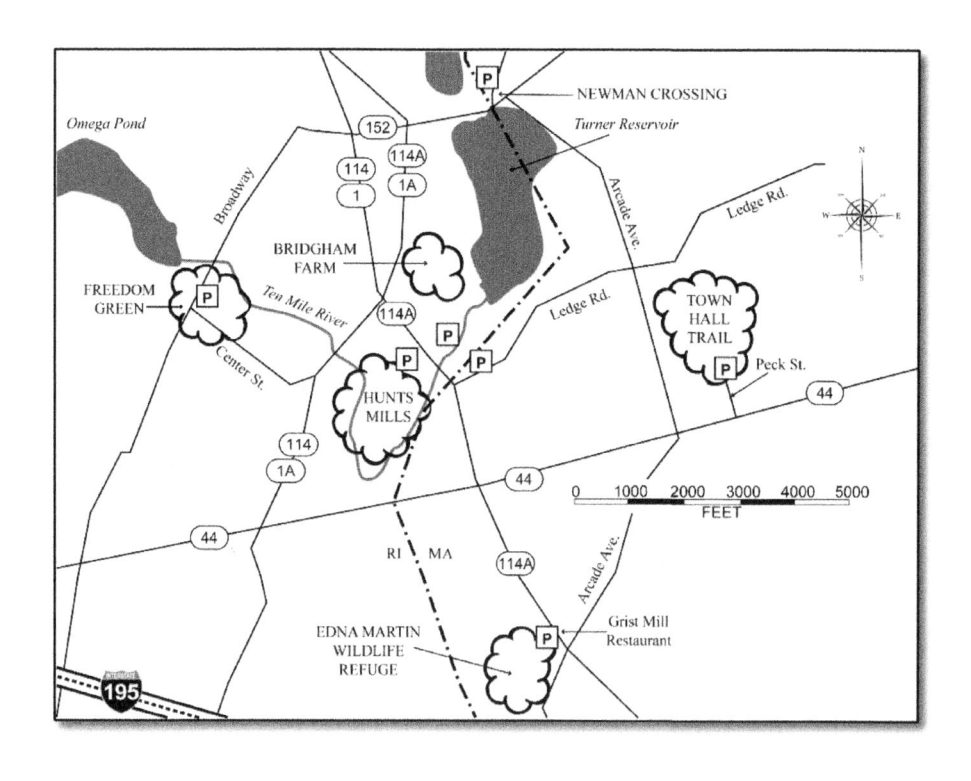

EAST PROVIDENCE

EAST PROVIDENCE

Bridgham Farm

Features: The Newman Oak, open meadow, access to Turner Reservoir loop trail.

Trail Map: N/A

GPS Coordinates: 41°50'02.81"N 71°20'33.69"W

Directions: Same access as Turner Reservoir, 400 Pleasant St. From intersection of Rts.95 and 195 in Providence, travel east on Rt.195 for 1.2 miles to the Rt.44 exit, heading northeast. Go 2 miles on Rt.44 to left onto Fall River Ave./Rt.114A. Follow Rt.114A north into East Providence 0.5 miles. Parking is on the right.

EAST PROVIDENCE

From Rt.152 in Seekonk, cross the state line into Rhode Island, (East Providence) and travel 0.5 miles to the next light (Rt.1A) turn left. Travel 0.5 miles to intersection with Rt.114A, at the light turn left onto Rt.114A, travel 0.3 miles to parking on the left. Look for trail kiosk.

Cost: Free.

Bathrooms: Not available.

Best Time to Visit: Year round.

Trail Conditions: Packed dirt path.

Distance: 0.75 miles.

Parking: On Rt.114A almost directly across from Hunts Mills road, same parking as Turner Reservoir. Room for about five cars. Additional, larger parking area due east 50 yards, just off Rt. 114A..

Access to this property is by way of the trail around the Turner Reservoir on the East Providence side of the Ten Mile River. After heading north and emerging from the woods on the west side of the reservoir,, look for the small opening into the field on the left, opposite the dam for the reservoir.

Bridgham Farm is a relatively small area for a walk and is a hidden gem in the suburbs. It is a large, former farm field with a few paths crossing it. In total there is about 0.75 miles of trail on this property, protected by the East Providence Land Conservation Trust. Once part of a much larger tract of land, this property was protected as open space and is all that remains of the colonial era farm.

In the summer months the field often has tall grass and some spots offer an abundance of milkweed. Bridgham Farm, listed on the National Historic Register, abuts the Turner Reservoir. At the end of the northerly most section of trail that leads through the woods to the nearby subdivision is the Newman Oak. This tree, a champion, is believed to be over 400 years old. The Ten Mile River Watershed Council usually hosts Full Moon Walks here in the spring and fall. (Ernie Germani, MTH)

EAST PROVIDENCE

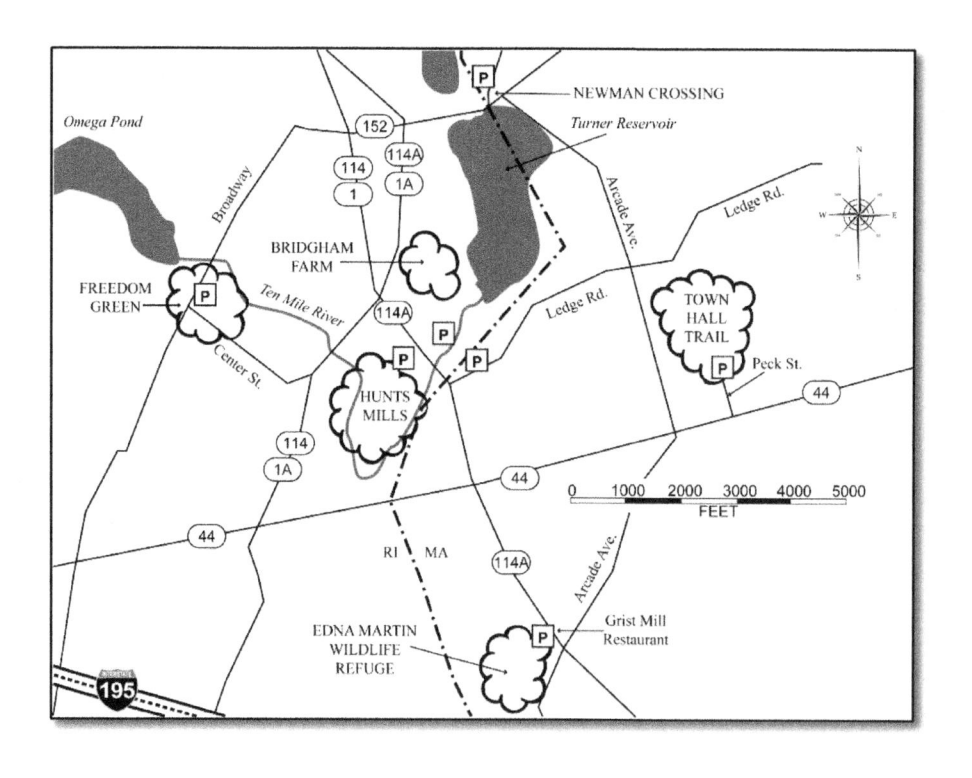

EAST PROVIDENCE

Freedom Green-Boat Trip

Features: Access to Ten Mile River canoe launch, paved walking path along Central Pond/Ten Mile River.

Trail Map: N/A

GPS Coordinates: 41°49'58.44"N 71°21'36.93"W

Directions: 1 Center St., Rumford. At corner of Center and North Broadway. From intersection of Rts.95 and 195,, travel eastbound on Rt.195 for 2 miles to the Warren Ave. exit, (north) then at 0.2 miles, turn right at the first light onto Broadway, go about 1.75 miles thru about 6 short lights and turn right on to Center St.

EAST PROVIDENCE

Cost: Free.

Bathrooms: Not available.

Best Time to Visit: Spring-fall.

Trail Conditions: Small park with paved sidewalk, to boat launch.

Distance: Approximately one mile to Hunt's Mills, by the Ten Mile River.

Parking: Space for six cars.

This is a river trip on the Ten Mile River which begins at Freedom Green Park in Rumford, RI. Follow the path beyond the gazebo to the launch near the bridge. Numerous civic events take place here throughout the year, none of which draw huge crowds. Several plaques in the park are dedicated to the victims of the 9/11 attack, and others have presidential quotes.

Freedom Green park is very near the area of the Roger Williams Trail, where the eventual founder of Rhode Island was told by the Massachusetts Bay Colony to vacate. He traveled by canoe down the Ten Mile River and across the Seekonk River to Providence where he found a more friendly environment.

At the launch you have the option to go right, upstream. Pass the Agawam Country club on the left and along some unobtrusive neighborhoods. Watch for flying golf balls and golf carts whose players wave as you paddle by. We were here in early June when the water was high and had a swift current. Paddling upstream in a kayak was not difficult. The area was fairly clean and lacked the pockets of litter that often pile up in urban rivers. A few sun turtles splashed into the water as we approached. The nearby golf course offered some beautiful views of the fairways.

In less than a mile, pass under the Pawtucket Ave. arch bridge and the nature of the shore alongside the river changes to dense woodland. Here are deep woods (it seems) even though the sound of road traffic is unavoidable. In this floodplain is a playground and ball field. The river often floods here in the spring. Vegetation is thick and trees often block the river, making passage tight and at times impassable.

We have made this trip several times and had to bump or wiggle off tree branches, adding a little more time to the trip. The shoreline here is no longer flat, instead it is steep in places.

At Otter Rock ledge along the way, someone in 1894 carved their initials when the area was an amusement park. After about a mile is a fork in the riveer; to the left is a raceway while the right leads to the Hunts Mills Dam and fish ladder. The dam and fish ladder are worth taking the time to stop and explore. John Hunt once ran a grist and saw mill in colonial times. In more modern times an amusement park was in this location as well as a pump station for a water supply. The massive stone building for the pump station still stands.

Returning downriver to Freedom Green offers the option to venture to Omega Pond or stop and come back to explore another day. We paddled to Omega Pond and the high dam and fish ladder which separate the Ten Mile from the Seekonk River, which is brackish. From

EAST PROVIDENCE

Freedom Green, pass under several road and railroad bridges which give the feeling of our not so distant industrial past. Bear to the left once and emerge into Omega Pond where a dam was built in the last century, long after Roger Williams' flight to Providence.

When we took this trip in June with high water, the quality of the pond water was tolerable. It was a long paddle across the pond to the outlet. In the quiet afternoon we heard barely a sound, and saw hardly a ripple on the pond. It was peaceful. We returned and marveled at the high railroad bridge and how it probably had served this area for decades. It was a great experience to explore an area so close to home, a place that is easy to take for granted. (Bill Luther)

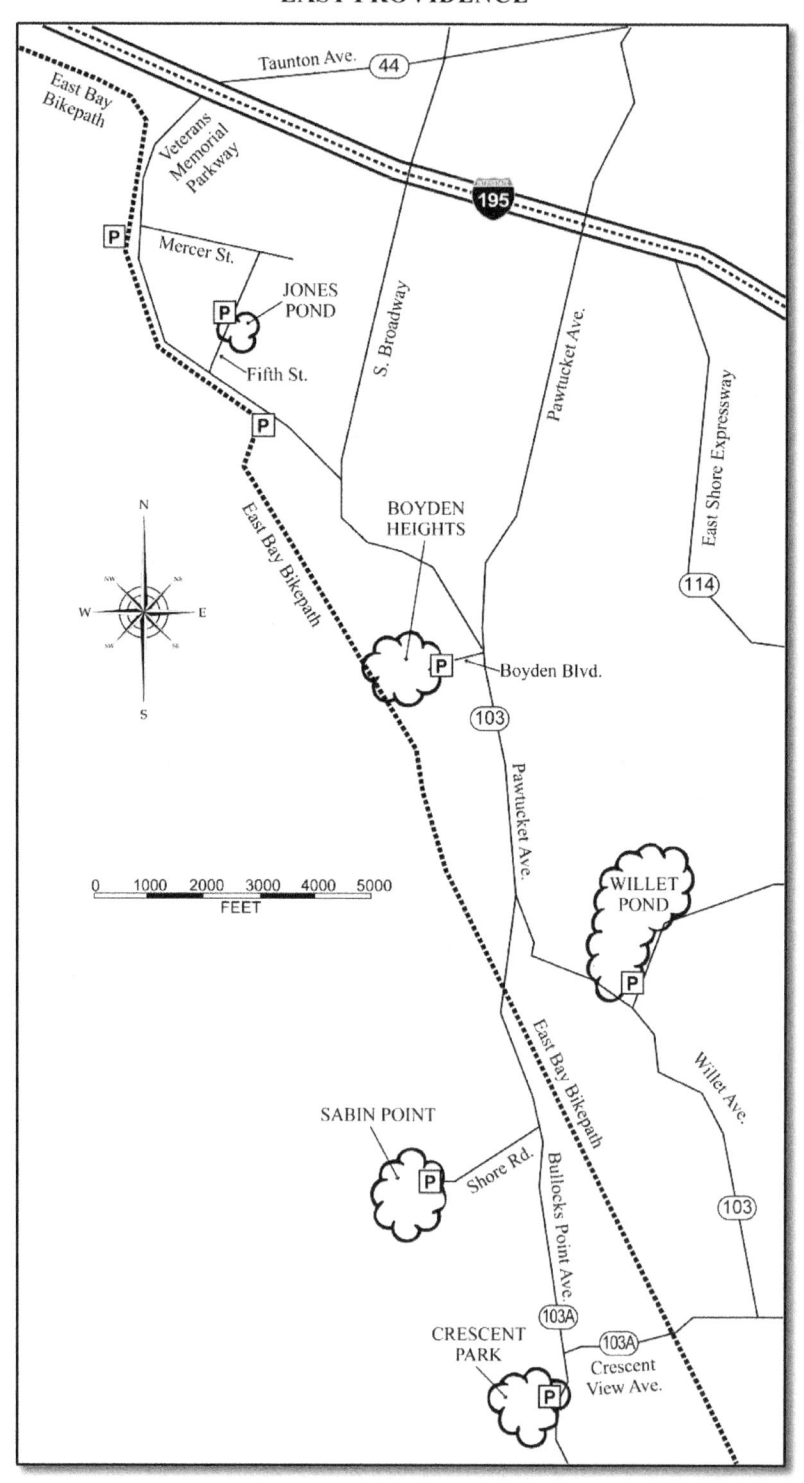

EAST PROVIDENCE

EAST PROVIDENCE

East Bay Bike Path

Features: Paved railtrail from Providence to Bristol, RI, ocean views. Trail travels through multiple state and town recreation areas.

Trail Map: Search "East Bay Bike path"

GPS Coordinates: (First parking south of Rt.195) 41°48'49.86"N 71°23'16.74"W

(Second parking area, across from Country Club) 41°48'11.77"N 71°22'54.82"W

EAST PROVIDENCE

Directions: 2 parking lots are available along Veterans Memorial Parkway in East Providence. From intersection of Rts.95 and 195 head east 0.6 miles to exit 4, Riverside, follow Veterans Memorial Parkway south 0.4 miles to parking lot on right. Second lot is 1.2 miles from Rt.195, also on Vets Parkway. Keep in mind the Rhode Island Department of Transportation (RIDOT) is changing exit numbers over the next few years! Vets Parkway does not have a route number. Use Riverside exit.

Cost: Free.

Bathrooms: Not available.

Best Time to Visit: Year round, not plowed in winter.

Trail Conditions: Paved bikeway along the east side of Narragansett Bay.

Distance: 13.8 miles from Providence to Bristol, RI.

Parking: India Point Park in Providence, two additional parking areas off Veteran's Memorial Parkway—parking closest to Rt.195 in East Providence is opposite Mercer Street, south is another lot opposite Metacomet Golf Club.

The East Bay Bike Path offers a terrific opportunity to walk or bike directly next to the ocean along the east side of Narragansett Bay. Numerous salt marshes draw birds and ducks of various types that swim just off shore. The path has some variety, not simply flat but with some small hills as well.

EAST PROVIDENCE

Most people who ride their bikes or walk on this railtrail have no idea they are passing through hundreds of years of history. This walk is not just miles of bike trail on a 10-foot-wide paved path with great views of the water, but more of a tour of yesteryear.

Starting at the picturesque Providence waterfront, the northern portion of the East Bay Bike Path leaves India Point Park and zigzags uphill toward the Washington Bridge. Over the years several bridges have been built over the Seekonk River. The first, built in 1793, was a covered drawbridge. The newly built George Redman Linear Park occupies what remains of the 1931 span. The bike path crosses the river through the linear park. There are several informational boards located here with a history of the bridges and surrounding neighborhoods.

After crossing the bridge, the bike path snakes down to Watchemoket Square in East Providence. Prior to the highway being built, the square was a bustling center of commerce and local government. It served as a crossroads where Taunton Ave. (Rt.44), Warren Ave. (Rt.6), and the railroad once met before crossing into Providence. The square was very active in the second half of the 19th century and well into the 20th century. Most of the buildings in the square were wood-framed buildings like that at the corner of Warren Ave. and First St. (currently the Black Duck Tavern). The predominant building remaining in the square was built in the early 1920's. The Neo-Federalist-designed building served as a bank for several years and is now the home of the Comedy Connection. Most of the remaining buildings in the square were torn down by the 1960's for the construction of Rt.195.

EAST PROVIDENCE

After crossing Warren Ave., the bike path follows First St. for two blocks before turning right and following alongside Veterans Memorial Parkway. This short section, about 0.2 miles, is the only stretch of road walking/biking. Beware of traffic. The next mile or so, the bike path first climbs up Fort Hill, past an overlook, and along the parkway before making its way to a former railroad bed. The fort on the hill, along with other fortifications in the area, protected Providence during the Revolutionary War and the War of 1812.

As the bike path climbs the top of the hill just before the lookout, you can see the Fort Hill Monument across the parkway. It is a large boulder near the intersection with Mercer Street. Winding around the first parking lot along the parkway, you now have a good vantage point of the Providence skyline. The buildings of downtown—Rhode Island Hospital, the Manchester Street Power Plant, and the I-way Bridge—are all clearly visible from here. In fact, in recent years, at 8:30 nightly people gather at this parking area along the bike path to shine their lights in the "Goodnight Hasbro" (Hasbro Children's Hospital) event.

The remaining distance of the bike path all the way to Bristol follows the rail bed that was once used by the Providence, Warren, and Bristol Railroad. As the bike path begins to follow the old rail bed, it is a causeway surrounded by water. To the right are the Providence River, and the Port of Providence. To the left is Watchemoket Cove, the first and largest of three coastal coves along this part of the bike path. All three of these coves are havens for birds and waterfowl.

After passing the first cove, the bike path passes over Kettle Point.

EAST PROVIDENCE

After passing the aptly named Long Rock Cove to the left, you come to a series of buildings on the right. They belong to the Squantum Association, and the largest building is the clubhouse. Built in 1900, it replaces the 1873 structure and is used for weddings and receptions.

The bike path passes next to another cove, which offers a long dock, which is part of the Boyden Heights Conservation Area. Just after the cove there is a trail that leads into the property. The trails here are short and would add a nice little hike to your walk.

Just after the trail head, the area to the left once hosted two amusement parks. Boyden Heights Park, opened in 1904, and Vanity Fair, opened in 1907, along with Crescent Park farther south. They gave this area the nickname "Coney Island of the East." Both of these amusement parks were closed by 1910.

The next portion of the bike path follows the waterfront and Ponham Rocks Lighthouse, which sits on one of two large rock islands and was built in 1871. Recent restoration has saved the lighthouse and a few times a year the island can be visited by the public. Search "Ponham Rocks boat tour" for information.

The bike path passes under Bullocks Point Ave. and comes out to Riverside Square. This was another bustling village back in the day, complete with a railroad station built in the mid- to late 1800's. Today the old depot is a coffee shop that is well worth a visit. Other buildings in the square also date back to yesteryear, but the most visited building here is the Dari-Bee, a local ice cream shop that is open from the spring to the fall. There are also a few "Mom & Pop" shops here as well,

EAST PROVIDENCE

including convenience stores for water or snacks. Also in the square is the Riverside World War II Memorial. It was originally located farther up the road and was relocated to the square in the early 2000's. The bike path, flanked by bird-filled shrubs, continues south passing through residential neighborhoods before coming to Bullocks Cove.

Looking north from the causeway as you cross the cove you can catch a glimpse of Little Neck, which is home to one of the oldest cemeteries in the nation. The cemetery, established in 1655, serves as the final resting place of several colonists including one who was a passenger on the Mayflower, as well as the first mayor of New York City. The cemetery is not accessible from the bike path.

The bike path then crosses Crescent View Ave. If you so choose, follow Crescent View Ave. west to its end. The 1895 Looff Carousel is the only remaining structure remaining of the once-bustling Crescent Park Amusement Park, which closed in the 1970's. After crossing Crescent View Ave., the bike path passes through another residential neighborhood, a small playground, and another small cove before reaching Haines State Park.

The bike path continues another eight miles to Bristol, passing through Barrington and Warren. (Ernie Germani, MTH)

EAST PROVIDENCE

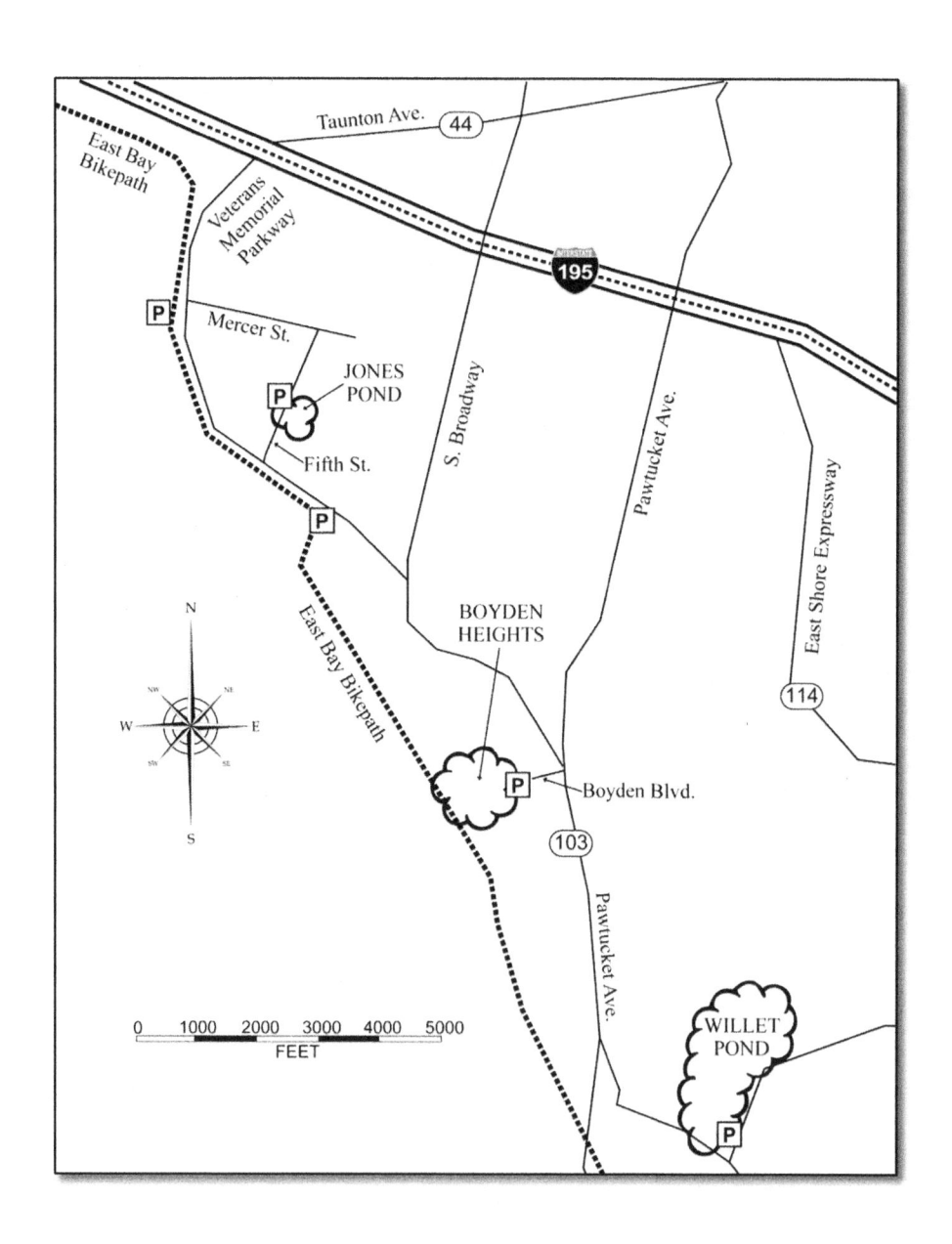

EAST PROVIDENCE

Boyden Heights

Features: Wooded trail out to boardwalk in wetland area bordering East Bay Bikepath, with access to the bike path.

Trail Map: N/A

GPS Coordinates: 41°47'22.38"N 71°22'10.48"W

EAST PROVIDENCE

Directions: 116 Boyden Blvd. From Rt.195 take exit 4 RIVERSIDE, follow Veterans Memorial Parkway to its end, continue south on Pawtucket Ave. (Rt.103) for 3 blocks. Boyden Blvd. is on the right. Follow Boyden Blvd. 0.2 miles, parking on right.

Cost: Free.

Bathrooms: Not available.

Best Time to Visit: Year round.

Trail Conditions: Challenging packed dirt, woodland path, boardwalk has railings and steps to allow for ease of access.

Distance: 0.75 miles out to boardwalk and back.

Parking: For 3–4 cars next to trail head at 116 Boyden Blvd.

Boyden Heights is an East Providence Conservation Commission property that overlooks a cove and the Providence River. The trail head starts at a small parking area on Boyden Blvd. A red-blazed loop trail, and a blue-blazed "lollipop" loop trail guide visitors through the area, as well as a few spurs that lead to the bike path on the property. It is small enough that you will not get lost if you choose to explore the entire property.

One of the highlights of Boyden Heights is the boardwalk. Swans, ducks, and several other species of birds, are commonly seen here. (Ernie Germani, MTH)

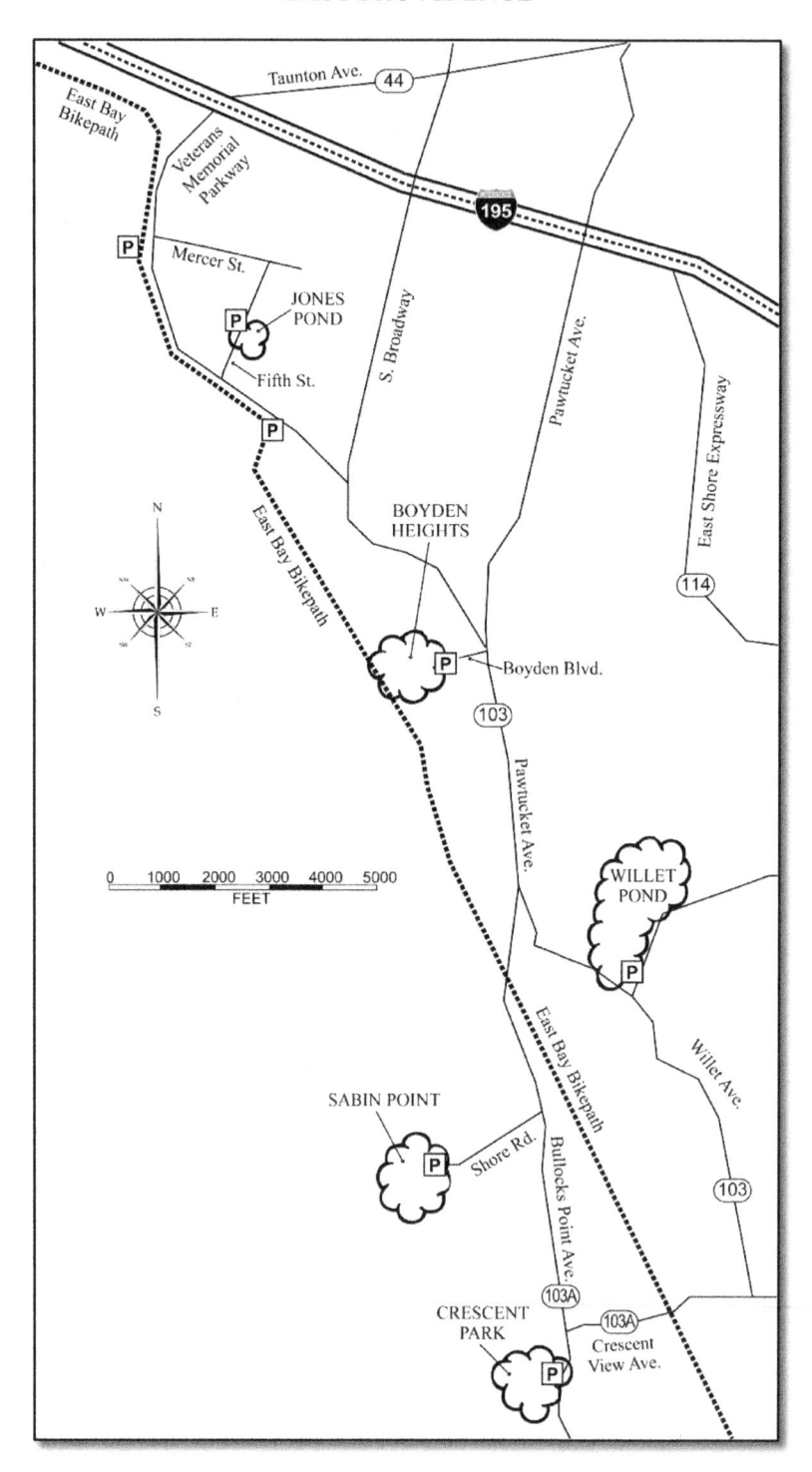

EAST PROVIDENCE

EAST PROVIDENCE

Sabin Point

Features: Shore access, views of Narragansett Bay, public boat launch. Presently no swimming allowed.

Trail Map: N/A

GPS Coordinates: 41°45'57.31"N 71°22'07.95"W

Directions: From intersection of Rts.95 and 195, travel east on Rt.195 for 0.6 miles, take exit 4 RIVERSIDE, follow Veterans Memorial Parkway to its end, 2.4 miles, continue south on

EAST PROVIDENCE

Pawtucket Ave. (Rt.103) for 1.5 miles, to right onto Shore Rd., drive 0.5 miles to park.

Cost: Free.

Bathrooms: Not available.

Best Time to Visit: Year round.

Trail Conditions: Cement walkways.

Distance: 0.5 miles loop walk around shore side park.

Parking: Two parking areas next to park, space for 10 cars.

Sabin Point offers magnificent views of Narragansett Bay, with walkways, playground, and a public boat launch. Spend an hour, or spend the day at the shoreline. The paved paths are easily accessible and allow ease of access to the ocean.

The point juts out into Narragansett Bay (actually the Providence River at this point) allowing for panoramic views. To the north the Port of Providence and the downtown skyline are visible. To the west and southwest you can see the shoreline of Warwick, and to the south you can see Conimicut Point and its lighthouse. The Ponham Rocks Light is also visible from Sabin Point. Until 1968, there was a lighthouse at Sabin Point. It is now marked by a day beacon. The river at Sabin Point is about a mile wide and is heavily used both for recreation and shipping. It is just as common to see large ships making their way to the Port of Providence as it to see a sailboat or speedboat.

EAST PROVIDENCE

The park features about a half mile of paved walking paths that are ADA accessible with curb cuts, basketball courts, and a playground among its trees and green grass. There is also a fishing dock and boat ramp here as well. It is a bustling little neighborhood park in the warmer months of the year. (Ernie Germani, MTH)

EAST PROVIDENCE

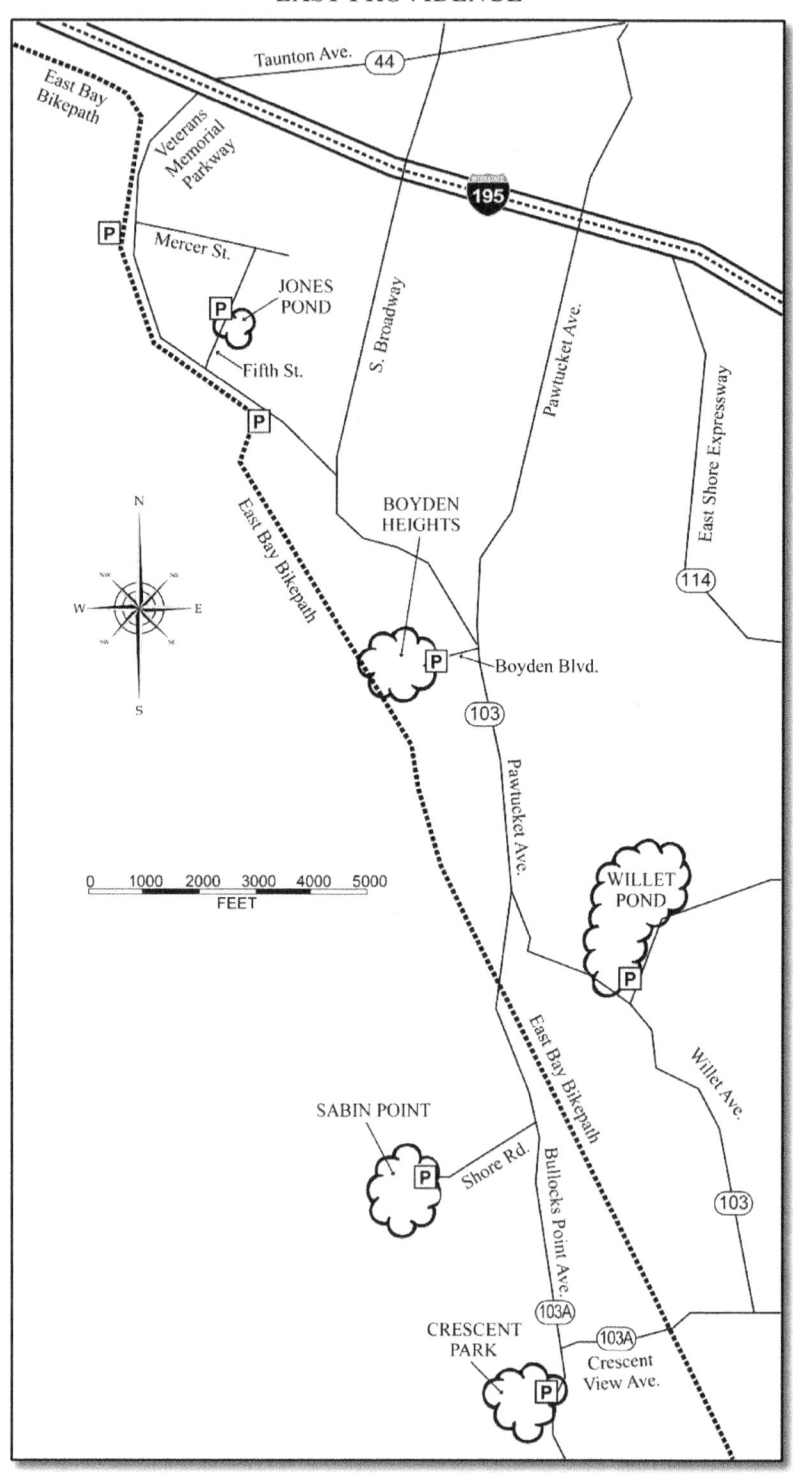

EAST PROVIDENCE

Crescent Park

Features: Shore access, ADA pathways to ocean views, carousel across the street in warm months (for fee).

Trail Map: N/A

GPS Coordinates: 41°45'21.99"N 71°21'36.55"W

Directions: From intersection of Rts.95 and 195, travel east 0.6 miles, take exit 4 RIVERSIDE, follow Veterans Memorial Parkway 2.5 miles to its end, continue south on Pawtucket Ave. (Rt.103) to intersection with Rt.103A (about 1 mile) bear right onto Rt.103A (Bullock's Point Ave.). Drive 1.6 miles. Just past Crescent View Ave., parking is on your right.

Cost: Free.

Bathrooms: Not available. In summer, near carousel.

Best Time to Visit: Year round.

Trail Conditions: Cement walkways.

Distance: 0.5 miles loop walk around shore side park.

Parking: Space for 20 cars.

Rose Larisa Park, commonly known as Crescent Park, in the Riverside section of East Providence, overlooks Narragansett Bay (actually the Providence River at this point). It is one of the city's newer parks, built in the 1990's. Today the park is crisscrossed with ADA accessible walking paths that wander through trees and large fields of grass. This property has a long history.

It was once a part of the larger Crescent Park, an amusement park that attracted visitors from all over the region. The shore dinner hall was located here. The large wall with the wrought iron fence was part of the back foundation of the building. A large dock stretched out into the river. Steamships from as far away as New York City docked here to drop off visitors to the park.

At low tide some of the remains of the pilings are visible below on

EAST PROVIDENCE

the beach. The majority of the park was across the street, including its midway and roller coaster. The amusement park began operations in the late 1800's and ceased in the late 1970's. The Looff Carousel was preserved and is still in operation today. This is a great park for the kids to run around in before catching a ride on the carousel, and the ocean views are stunning. (Ernie Germani, MTH)

EAST PROVIDENCE

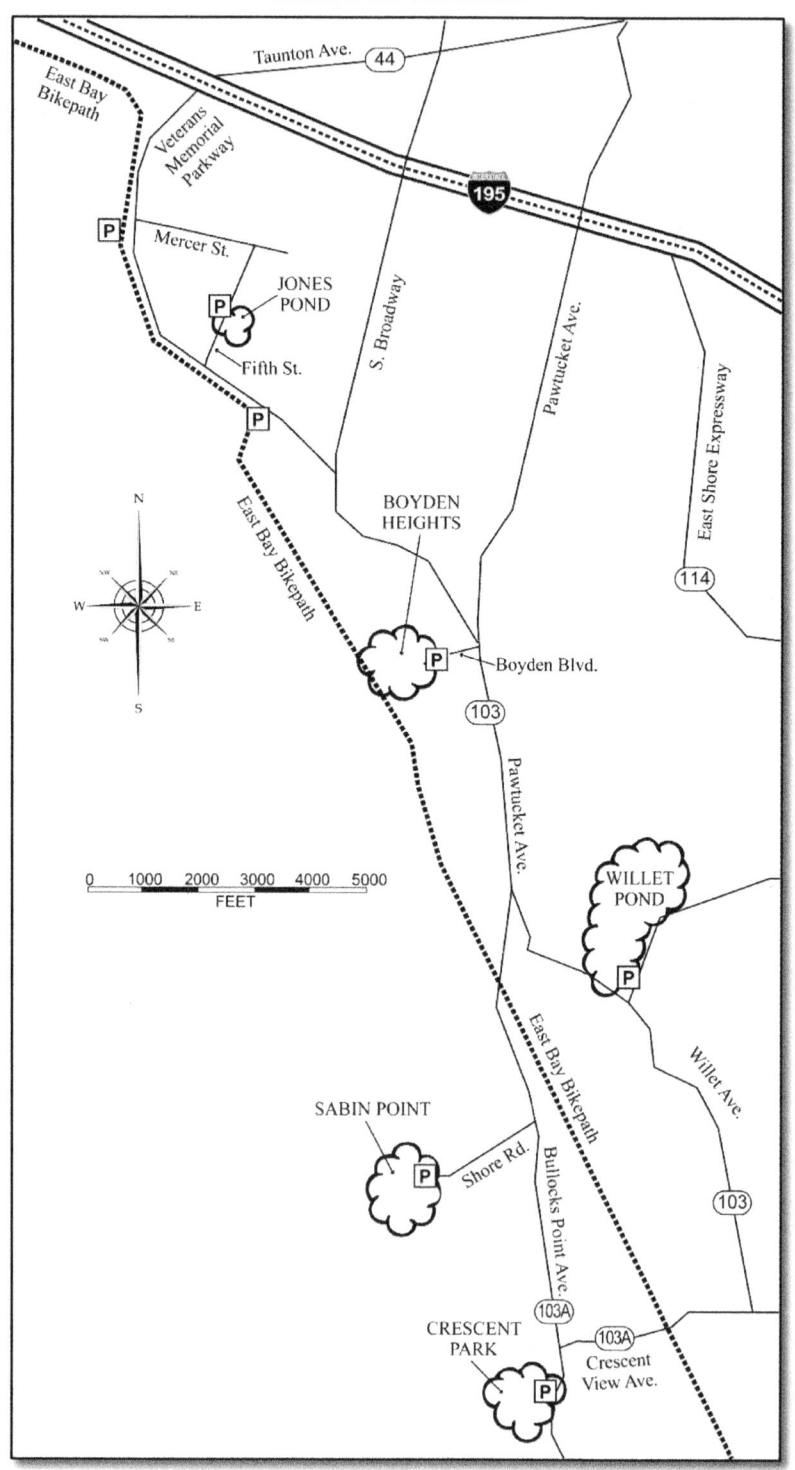

EAST PROVIDENCE

Willett Pond

Features: Loop trail, canoe launch, water views.

Trail Map: N/A

GPS Coordinates: 41°46'30.70"N 71°21'22.98"W

Directions: 204 Willett Ave. From Rt.195 east take exit 4 Riverside, follow Veterans Memorial Parkway to junction with Rt.103 (2.5 miles), continue south on Pawtucket Ave. (Rt.103), continue 1 mile to a left onto Willett Ave. Travel 0.3 miles, look for pond on your left, park behind stores adjacent to the pond.

Cost: Free.

Bathrooms: Not available.

Best Time to Visit: Year round.

Trail Conditions: Packed dirt, clearly blazed loop trail.

Distance: 0.5 mile loop walk around Willett Pond.

Parking: Behind Shroder's Deli on Willett Ave.

Willett Pond was used in the past as an ice pond. Industrious workmen cut cakes of ice in the winter and stored the ice blocks in an ice house for use in the hot summer months.

These days the only ice you'll see is formed naturally, and will remain in the pond till spring. A small canoe launch allows fishermen or kayakers to paddle about on this small pond. Houses line one side of the pond, but the trail around the pond is all on City of East Providence property, and you are welcome to access the entire loop trail. Follow the orange blaze markers. (Ernie Germani, MTH)

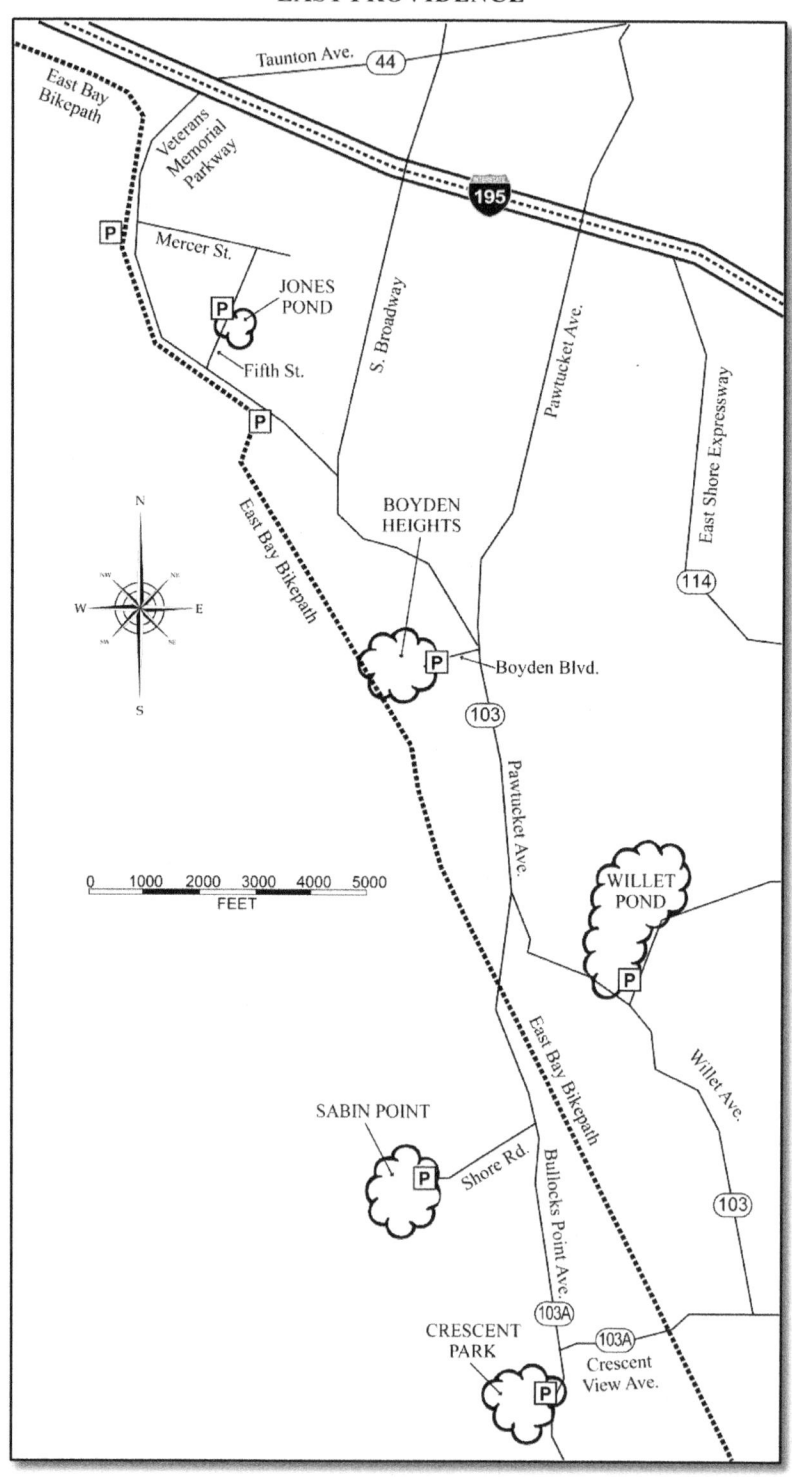

EAST PROVIDENCE

EAST PROVIDENCE

Jones Pond

Features: Short loop trail around pond.

Trail Map: N/A

GPS Coordinates: 41°48'31.82"N 71°23'06.60"W

Directions: From Intersection of Rts.95 and 195, travel east on Rt.195 to exit 4, Riverside, and take Veterans Memorial Parkway, head south on the parkway for just under 1 mile, look on your left

EAST PROVIDENCE

for Fifth St. Turn left onto Fifth St., drive 0.1 mile to parking on the right next to pond. Jones Pond is directly next to Pierce Field.

Cost: Free.

Bathrooms: Not available.

Best Time to Visit: Year round.

Trail Conditions: Crushed stone dust walkways.

Distance: 0.5 miles of walkways around small pond.

Parking: Next to Pierce Field on Fifth St. for about 5 cars.

Tucked away in a suburban neighborhood is a new walking path in a revitalized park. Jones Pond has a long history for a small park. Originally a freshwater kidney-shaped pond, it is said to be the location of a Native American village, according to an old book by The Narragansett Archaeological Society of Rhode Island. In the early 20th century a quarry was also nearby.

During the 1930's the adjacent Pierce Field Stadium was constructed and Jones Pond was "squared off" to the shape it is today. During World War II, Quonset huts were built and used on the property. For years after that the pond served as a neighborhood spot for ice skating before falling into disarray. Recently the pond and surrounding park have been given new life with a half mile of walking paths with perennial gardens. Look for the rather interesting and artistic bike racks here. The small shrubs and trees serve as a haven for several species of birds.

During Fourth of July festivities this area is closed to the public since it is the launch site for East Providence's fireworks display. (Ernie Germani, MTH)

Pawtucket

PAWTUCKET

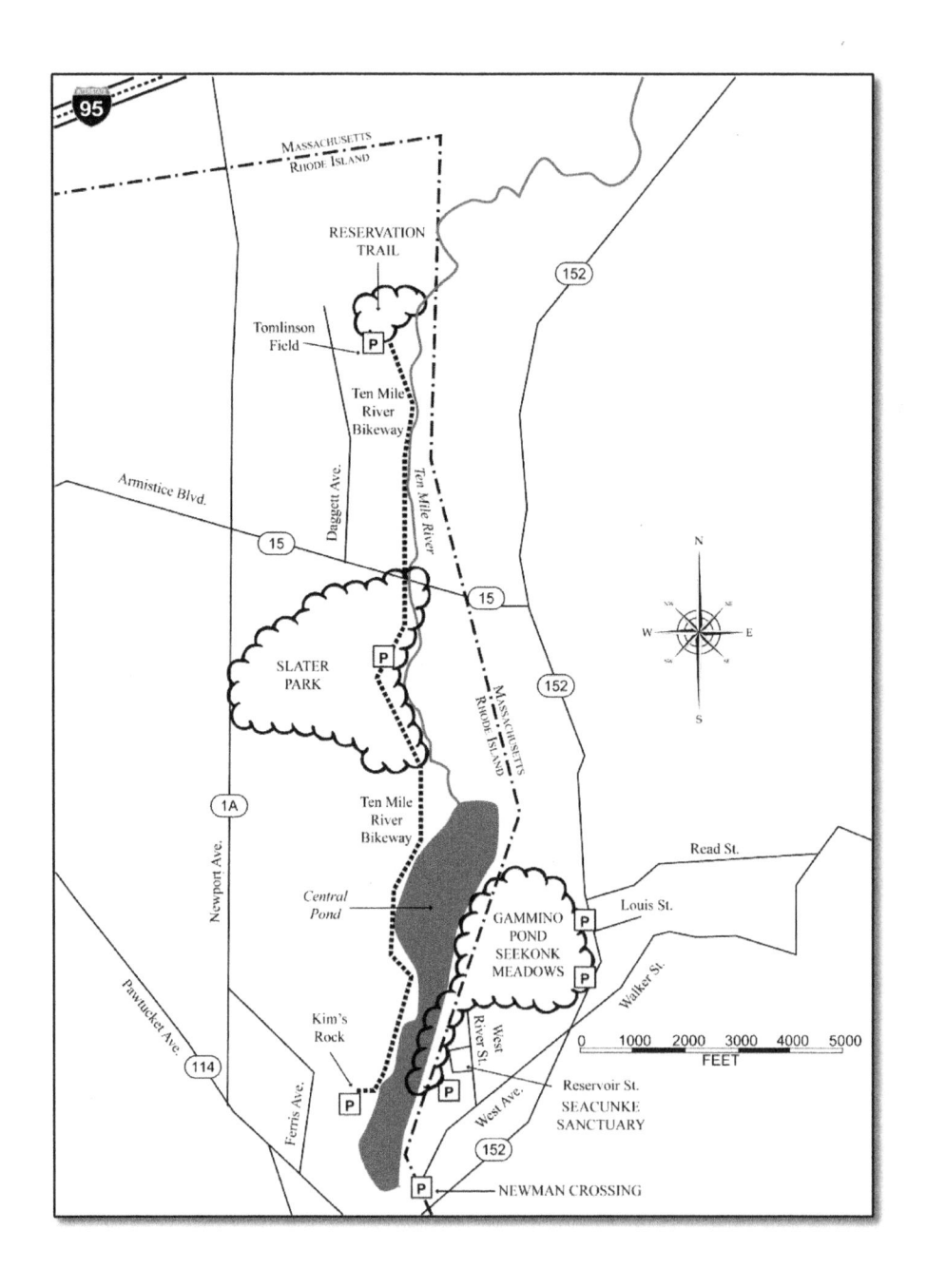

PAWTUCKET

Ten Mile River Greenway

Features: Paved bike path along Central Pond/Ten Mile River.

Trail Map: Search "ridot ten mile river greenway map"

GPS Coordinates: Tomlinson Field 41°53'07.19"N 71°20'42.73"W

Slater Park 41°52'07.85"N 71°21'14.67"W

Kim's Rock (East Providence) 41°50'52.49"N 71°20'45.58"W

Directions: Three access points, **Tomlinson Field, Pawtucket**: From intersection of Rts.95 and 1A, exit at 2A, Newport Ave., (Rt.1A) to head south on 1A in S. Attleboro for 1 mile to left onto

PAWTUCKET

Central Ave., travel 0.3 miles to Daggett Ave. on the right, turn right, Tomlinson Field entrance is 0.3 miles down on the left.

Slater Park, Pawtucket; 426 Newport Ave. Rt.95 south to Newport Ave., Attleboro, exit 2A, (Rt.1A) for 2 miles to Park entrance on left. Or from Rt.95, follow Rt.1A south for 1.5 miles to left onto Armistice Blvd., travel 0.5 miles, alternate park entrance is on the right.

Kim's Rock Field, East Providence: From intersection of Rts.95 and 195, head east on Rt.195 to Rt.44 exit, travel on Rt.44 for 2 miles (Rt.44 becomes one-way). At intersection with Rt.114A, Pawtucket Ave., turn left. Drive 0.75 miles to intersection with Rts.1A and 114A, bear to the right to stay on Rt.1A northbound (Pawtucket Ave.). In 0.5 miles, at intersection with Rt.152, drive straight through intersection, then take an immediate sharp right onto Ferris Ave. Entrance to Kim's Rock Field is 0.5 miles down on Ferris Ave., on the right. Entrance to bikeway is at the back of the field.

Cost: Free

Bathrooms: Not available.

Best Time to Visit: Spring through fall—not plowed in winter.

Trail Conditions: Paved bike path with very small hills.

Distance: Three miles, one way.

Parking: Tomlinson Field, Pawtucket; Slater Park, Pawtucket, Kim's Rock, East Providence.

PAWTUCKET

The Ten Mile River Greenway is three miles in length and winds along the shores of Central Pond and the Ten Mile River north from East Providence into Pawtucket. The southern section of the bike path starts at Kimberly Rock Field, has a few easy hills, and offers several side trails that lead to the picturesque shores of Central Pond.

From Kimberly Rock Field to Slater Park is just about a mile and a half. Geese, swans, ducks, and rabbits are quite commonly seen along this stretch. For the next 0.3 miles the bike path follows the river as it passes through man-made canals built during the Great Depression.

This area is part of Slater Park, the pride and joy of the Pawtucket park system. The bike path then crosses busy Armistice Boulevard. On the right is a small dam and waterfall with a pond behind it. The bike path passes between this pond to the right and the Darlington neighborhood to the left before ending at Tomlinson Field along Daggett Ave. (Ernie Germani)

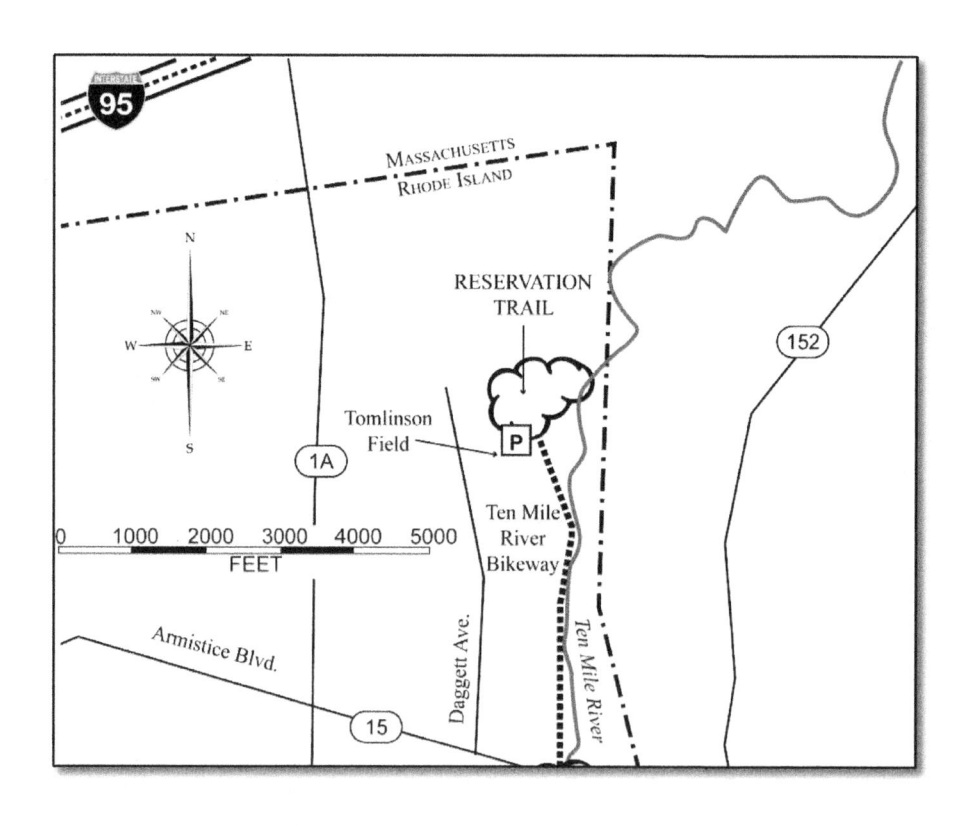

PAWTUCKET

PAWTUCKET

Reservation Trail

Features: Small pond, wooded trail just off Ten Mile River Greenway, access to shores of Central Pond.

Trail Map: N/A

GPS Coordinates: 41°53'07.19"N 71°20'42.73"W

Directions: Tomlinson Field, Daggett Blvd. From intersection of Rts.95 and 1A, exit, travel south on Newport Ave. (Rt.1A) for 1 mile to left onto Central Ave., travel 0.3 miles to Daggett Ave. on the right, turn right, Tomlinson Field entrance is 0.3 miles down on the left.

Cost: Free.

PAWTUCKET

Bathrooms: Not available.

Best Time to Visit: Year round.

Trail Conditions: Unmarked packed dirt trail out to Ten Mile River.

Distance: 0.5 miles

Parking: At back of Tomlinson Field.

At the north end of the Ten Mile River Greenway a wooded area abuts the shores of the Ten Mile River. The out-and-back primitive trail runs northerly toward the ruins of Lebanon Mills.

The trail, a work in progress, is being improved by members of the Ten Mile River Watershed Council. Blazes have recently been added along parts of the trail. From the parking area at Tomlinson Field, make your way down the bike path a few hundred feet. A trail head is visible to the left. Turn and follow it and stay to the right at the trail split.

The trail comes to a large open area by a pond. Stay to the right and make your way slightly uphill and to the left. You will come to the well-defined trail once again. From here the trail is easy to follow as it skirts the shores of the river to its end at the ruins of Lebanon Mills. The trail may be wet in places. (Ernie Germani, MTH)

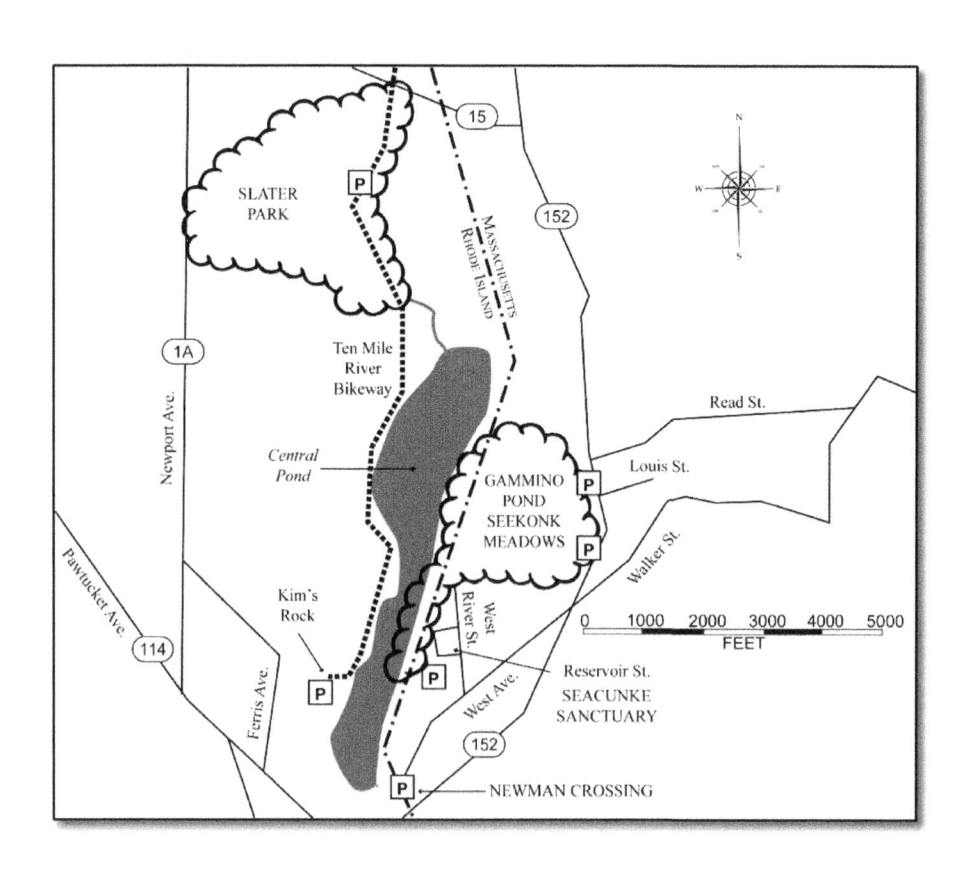

PAWTUCKET

PAWTUCKET

Slater Park

Features: Ten Mile River Greenway at back edge of park, extensive ADA walking paths, multiple parking areas, Looff Carousel, Daggett Farm, duck pond, holiday lights display.

Trail Map: Search "Pawtucket parks and Rec Slater Park"

GPS Coordinates: 41°52'07.85"N 71°21'14.67"W

Directions: 426 Newport Ave. From Rt.95 in S. Attleboro take exit 2A south on Newport Ave Attleboro, (Rt.1A) for 2 miles to Park entrance on left. Or from Rt.95, follow Rt.1A south for 1.5 miles to

PAWTUCKET

Armistice Blvd, Rt.15, turn left, travel on Armistice Blvd. for 0.5 miles, alternate park entrance is on the right.

Cost: Free for park and Daggett farm, small fee for carousel.

Bathrooms: Available seasonally.

Best Time to Visit: Year round, Daggett Farm open 9 a.m.–3:30 p.m. Remainder of park open 7 a.m.—9 p.m. Carousel open in summer.

Trail Conditions: Paved walking paths, paved bike trail through back edge of park alongside Central Pond.

Distance: 0.8 miles

Parking: Throughout park, on street, and dedicated parking areas.

Slater Park is the crown jewel of Pawtucket's parks. In recent years the park has undergone a renaissance with Daggett Farm essentially replacing the former Slater Park Zoo. Daggett Farm is housed within the park, and offers therapeutic and disability-friendly gardening areas. The park has also become home to the Pawtucket Arts Festival.

Summer brings the tradition of the Looff Carousel, which has been in operation at the park for over one hundred years. Take a ride on the carousel for a small fee, and allow yourself to enjoy the feeling of riding back into history.

In the holiday season the park is decorated and very festive. The park also has several walking paths and the Ten Mile River Greenway

PAWTUCKET

Bike Path skirts the eastern, back edge of the park. One of the most recognizable features of the park is the pond and bandstand. (Ernie Germani, MTH)

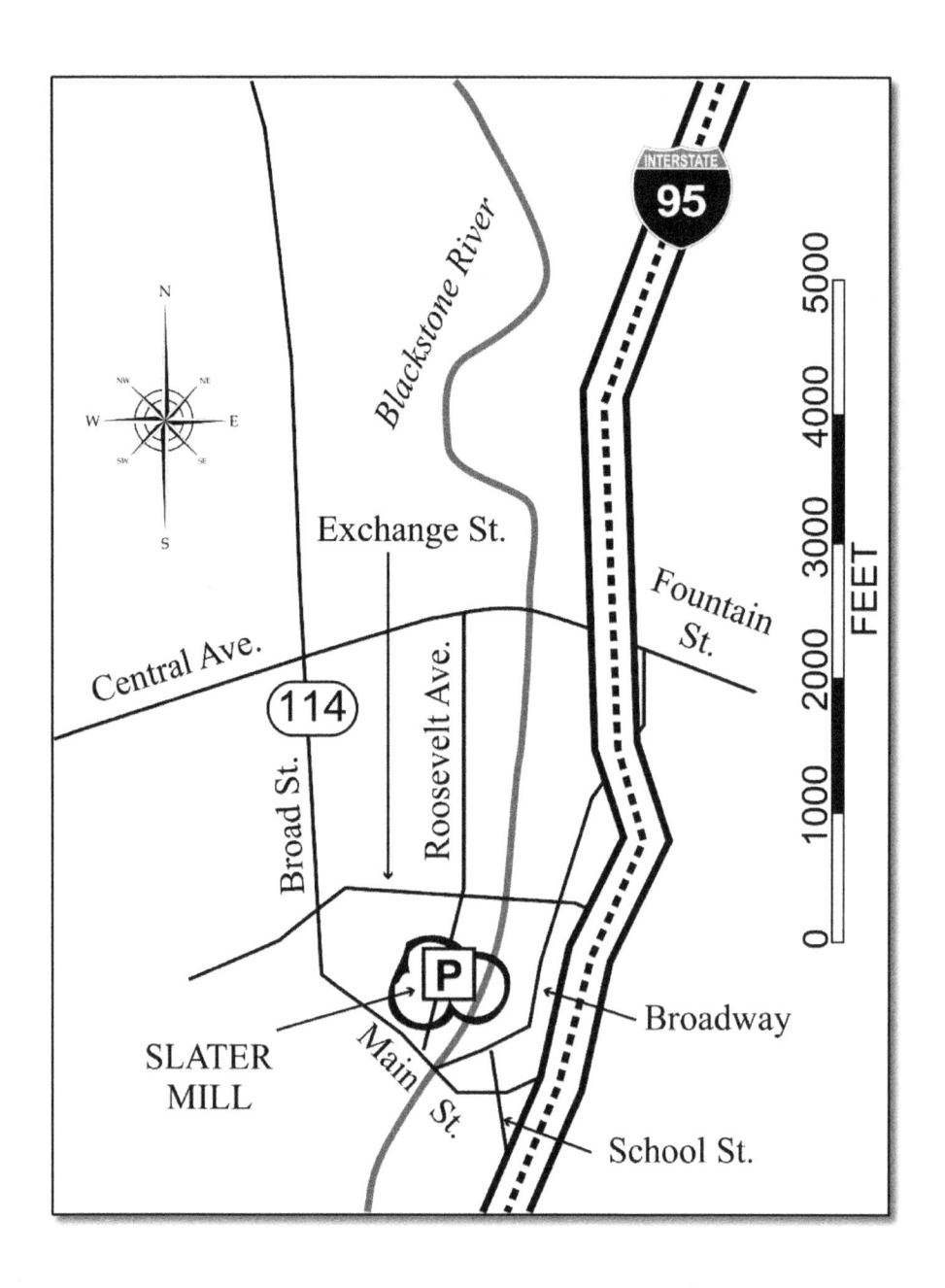

PAWTUCKET

PAWTUCKET

Slater Mill

Features: Views of Blackstone River, portion of Blackstone River Bikeway, Slater Mill Museum, Visitor's Center for Blackstone Valley National Historic Park.

Trail Map: N/A

GPS Coordinates: 41°52'40.86"N 71°22'58.49"W

Directions: 67 Roosevelt Ave., Pawtucket. **From the south**, take Rt.95 North to exit 28 for School St. Turn left off the ramp on

PAWTUCKET

School St. for 0.2 miles. Drive through traffic light, bear left on Broadway, then right on Main St. Turn right on Roosevelt Ave. **From the north**, take Rt.95 South to exit 29 for Downtown Pawtucket. Turn right onto Fountain St., drive 0.4 miles to right on Exchange St. for 0.1 mile, then left on Roosevelt Ave. for 0.1 mile to parking on the left, just past Pawtucket City Hall.

Cost: Free.

Bathrooms: Available at Blackstone Valley National Historic Park's Visitor's Center.

Best Time to Visit: Year round for walking, Slater Mill Museum open March to Nov., 10 a.m.–4 p.m., Dec.–Feb. by appointment. Blackstone Valley National Historic Park Visitor's Center open M-Sat. 10 a.m.–4 p.m., Sun. 11 a.m.–4 p.m.

Trail Conditions: Paved walking paths, cobblestone pathways, paved 0.25 mile bike trail behind Pawtucket City Hall.

Distance: 0.5 mile.

Parking: Municipal parking next to City Hall, additional parking next to historic buildings of Slater Mill, adjacent to the Blackstone River. More parking next to Blackstone Valley National Historic Park Visitor's Center, across the street.

The historic buildings alongside the Blackstone River where Samuel Slater erected his first industrial weaving mills are the southern terminus for the Blackstone Valley National Historic Park. Historic

PAWTUCKET

buildings constructed next to the river tell the history of the development of industrialization in America, spurred by the inventions of Samuel Slater.

In 1793, on the banks of the Blackstone River, Samuel Slater built and began operating the first water-powered cotton-thread spinning factory in America, which launched the industrial revolution in this country. The Blackstone Valley National Historic Park seeks to tell the story of how industry has transformed the Blackstone Valley, and ultimately, much of the rest of the country, for better and for worse. The many dams along rivers and streams throughout this area reflect the need for sources of power. On our walks in woodland areas we often encounter remnants of small dams that were built to create local sources of power for local enterprises.

We are still living with the results of rapid and sometimes thoughtless development. Our rivers, especially the Blackstone, as well as the Ten Mile River and many others, were often used as both sewage disposal systems and places to flush out industrial waste from the many operations that located next to rivers. Waterways were used both as a source of power, and also as a source of easy waste disposal. Eating fish taken from these rivers is not advised. The fish are contaminated with heavy metals that settled in the sediment of these hard-working rivers.

Wildlife, however, has not gotten the message about the heavy metals present in the river sediment. There is no shortage of birds and other wildlife along the banks of these rivers. Take in the sights and sounds of the river, and learn more of the history of this area when you

PAWTUCKET

visit this remarkable spot along the Blackstone River in Pawtucket. (MTH, Ernie Germani)

Acknowledgments

Thanks to all members of the Ten Mile River Watershed Council, past and present, who supported this project. All content contributors are acknowledged at the end of each chapter in which they had a part. Sue Stephenson (AKA Auntie Beak) provided book design as a gift to the Watershed Council.

Thanks for the enthusiastic letters of support written by Bill Harley and Debbie Block of Seekonk; Chris Yarworth, Conservation Agent in Plainville; Marcia Szymanski, Director of *New Hope* in Attleboro; Shannon Palmer, Conservation Agent in N. Attleboro; and Shane Hanlon of Foxboro.

"This publication is supported in part by a grant from the Seekonk, North Attleboro, and Plainville, MA Cultural Councils, local agencies which are supported by the Mass Cultural Council, a state agency."

Editor's Note

Thank you for reading this book. It's always thrilling to learn that readers have been able to use the information we've worked so hard to share. It's even nicer when we hear that this publication has encouraged families to get outside to spend time together in the outdoors.

Take a minute to write a review

If you found this book to be useful, please take the time to tell others about it. A review posted on Amazon is a real gift, whether you loved the book or have a criticism.

Keep in touch

Be sure to visit the "Ten Mile River Watershed Council" at our website, www.tenmileriver.net, email us at info@tenmileriver.net or visit our Facebook page "Ten Mile River Watershed Council" to learn about group events—river cleanups, walks, groups paddles, and more. Come on over and "like" the *Easy Walks in Massachusetts* Facebook page or www.marjorieturner.com to see what Marjorie Turner Hollman is up to next.

Made in United States
North Haven, CT
27 April 2023